PERENNIALS

RICHARD ROSENFELD

**LONDON, NEW YORK,
MUNICH, MELBOURNE, DELHI**

Series Editor Zia Allaway
Series Art Editor Alison Donovan
Managing Editor Anna Kruger
Managing Art Editor Lee Griffiths
Consultant Louise Abbott
DTP Designer Louise Waller
Media Resources Richard Dabb, Lucy Claxton
Picture Research Bridget Tily
Production Controller Mandy Inness
US Editor Christine Heilman
US Senior Editor Jill Hamilton
US Editorial Assistant John Searcy

Produced on behalf of Dorling Kindersley by
HILTON/SADLER
Editorial director: Jonathan Hilton
Design director: Peggy Sadler

Introduction Text Zia Allaway

First American Edition, 2003

Published in the United States by
DK Publishing, Inc.
375 Hudson Street
New York, New York 10014

05 10 9 8 7 6 5 4

A Cataloging-in-Publication record for this book
is available from the Library of Congress.

ISBN 0-7894-9344-6

Color reproduction by Colourscan, Singapore
Printed and bound in Italy by Printer Trento

discover more at
www.dk.com

Gardening with perennials

OR A GARDEN OVERFLOWING with flowers and foliage from spring to summer to autumn, plant it with perennials. Feathery ferns, free-flowering cranesbills, and tall, spiky phormiums all fall within this group, their exquisite beauty and reliability combining to make them among the most popular of all garden plants. Most perennials are easy to care for too, popping up year after year to adorn beds, borders, and containers. Their versatility and variety of flower and form make an invaluable contribution to any design, from a traditional cottage garden to a modern minimalist roof terrace.

To understand how to use perennials in your garden, it's helpful to know how they grow. A perennial is a plant that lives for more than three years and produces herbaceous, or soft, growth that doesn't become woody like the stems of shrubs and trees. Most perennials die down in winter and the topgrowth reappears the following spring. Although this factor must be considered when creating a garden where interest is required year-round, with careful planning, you can include evergreen perennials and those that flower very early and late in the year to keep the show going.

◀ **Electric blue corydalis** brightens up borders from early spring to summer.

▶ **Easy to grow and free-flowering**, cranesbills quickly pay for themselves.

Naturalistic planting styles

The beauty of perennials is that they suit all gardens, large and small, and can be used in many different designs. For a romantic cottage garden, select a medley of colors and forms, and try mixing perennials with annuals and shrub roses to create flower-filled borders that have a random, naturalistic look. Excellent choices for this style include poppies, daisylike coreopsis, lupins, and tall delphiniums.

Waves of color and form are created in a prairie garden, which combines grasses and perennials.

Another natural gardening design style, known as "prairie planting," uses perennials to mimic the way plants grow in the wild. A limited number of species is planted in large, informal swaths, with one variety blending seamlessly into the next, creating waves of color and texture.

Prairie planting also relies heavily on grasses, such as *Miscanthus sinensis* and *Calamagrostis*, which soften the contours of the planting. When left to stand over winter, their dried stems and flower spikes provide structure after

A dusting of frost on faded sedum flowers offers late autumn interest.

other perennials have died down. Breaking with formal gardening convention, tall "see-through" plants, such as *Verbena bonariensis*, with its slim stems topped by buttons of purple flowers, are often planted in front of shorter plants. This blurs the focus and gives prairie-style gardens an almost dreamlike quality.

Diminutive evergreen grasses planted in clay pots contrast well with summer perennials, such as hostas.

Formal gardens

Perennials are equally effective in wild and natural gardens or formal spaces. The hard lines of a geometric lawn or paved area are softened by flowing borders filled with perennials. A simple plan and limited palette will produce the most elegant designs. A garden filled with just white or blue plants is a classic example of a formal scheme, although even bright pinks or oranges work well when used in moderation and offset by cooler tones.

Modern spaces

Contemporary gardens can also be enriched with perennials. Sculptural shrubs form the basis of many modern designs, but the subtle shapes and colors of perennials can be good foils for modern building materials. A long

Perennials look at home in a traditional garden, while large swaths of plants offer a modern twist.

border of catmint (*Nepeta sibirica*) set against a simple wall will inject texture and color, and create an evolving shadow display as the sun moves across the sky. Tall irises offer distinctive flowers in early summer and architectural foliage over a long period.

This book includes some of the best and most reliable perennials. Knowing your hardiness zone will help you choose the ones that will flourish in your area. The United States Department of Agriculture has produced a map of hardiness zones, which is based on average annual minimum temperatures; this map can be found on their web site (http://www.usda.gov).

Contemporary features, such as smooth plastered walls, provide a perfect foil for soft, informal perennials.

Choosing perennials

WITH SO MANY PERENNIALS to choose from, it's easy to find one that suits the site and soil in your garden and fits the style and planting plan. Before buying, always check the plant for signs of disease or poor growth, and only select healthy specimens. The checklist below will help you to make a good choice.

Strong, healthy
topgrowth

Disease-free,
vigorous leaves

Moist soil mix,
free of weeds
and moss

Established,
vigorous roots

Potbound roots
Before buying a plant, make sure its roots have not become constricted or potbound. This will cause poor growth, since it limits a plant's ability to take in nutrients and water.

Planting perennials

The beauty of container-grown perennials is that they can be planted at almost any time of year, as long as the soil is not waterlogged or frozen, although the best times are spring and autumn. In autumn, the soil tends to be wet and warm, enabling perennials to establish roots quickly before the onset of winter. In some areas, spring planting is better for perennials that do not like cold, wet conditions. Planting in drier summer months requires more aftercare, since you will need to water your plants well until they are established. Before planting, make sure the soil is weed-free.

1 Preparing the planting hole

Water the plant thoroughly before planting. Dig a hole 1½ times wider and a little deeper than the root ball. Then water the hole and allow it to drain. Holding the stems between your fingers, tip the plant out of its pot.

2 Teasing out the roots

Mix the removed soil with some well-rotted compost, and add some more compost to the bottom of the planting hole. If the roots are coiled around the sides of the pot, tease them out very carefully.

3 Planting and finishing off

Place the plant in the hole with its crown at the correct depth, which is usually the same as it was in its pot (see overleaf). Gradually backfill around the plant with the mix of soil and compost, firming gently as you go.

Planting depths

To get your plants off to a good start, make sure they are planted at
the correct depth. The majority should be planted at the same level
as they were in their pots, but some prefer their crowns (where the
stems meet the roots) to sit in the damp soil below the surface.
Others will rot unless their crowns are set above the soil.

Crown level with
soil surface

Crown 1in (2.5cm)
below the soil level

Crown above
ground level

Crown 4in (10cm)
below the soil

Ground-level planting
Most perennials, including
this New England aster,
are planted at ground
level. This means that the
crown is level with the soil
surface, as it would have
been in its original pot.

Shallow planting
Shallow planting is best
for perennials that need
moist soil, such as this
hosta. Shallow-plant by
positioning the crown
1in (2.5cm) below the
surface of the soil.

Deep planting
Perennials with tuberous
root systems, such as this
polygonatum, often need
to be planted deeply. Set
the crown at about 4in
(10cm) below the soil
surface for good results.

Raised planting
Perennials that are prone
to rotting at the base,
or have variegated foliage
that may revert to green,
like this sisyrinchium, are
planted with the crown
just above ground level.

Caring for perennials

PERENNIALS ARE GENERALLY low-maintenance plants. Once established, they only need watering during dry periods and prompt removal of encroaching weeds. If you apply an organic mulch, such as well-rotted compost, over the soil, these jobs become even easier. A mulch suppresses weeds, keeps moisture in the soil, and slowly releases nutrients. This just leaves you to pick off the fading blooms.

Watering perennials
Water newly planted perennials regularly, even those that like dry soil. Once the roots are developed, watering regimens vary, depending on the plant and soil.

Improving flowering

Extend the flowering period of your perennials using the following methods. Removing flowers before they go to seed stimulates a plant to produce more blooms. Also, for a bushier plant, thin out spindly and weak shoots in spring to encourage new stems to develop from the base.

Pinching out
When plants reach one-third of their final height, pinch out the stem tips to encourage sideshoots to develop.

Deadheading
Encourage more flowering shoots to develop by removing flowers as soon as they start to fade.

Cutting back
After flowering, when new shoots are visible at the base, cut back the flowered stems to ground level.

Propagating perennials

THERE ARE MANY WAYS to propagate new plants from old. Growing perennials from seed or dividing clumps in spring or autumn are simple methods, although taking stem or root cuttings is also easy. Plants raised from seed may not flower for two years or more.

Growing perennials from seed

It's cheap and easy to grow large numbers of perennials from seed. When collecting the seeds yourself, take them only from strong plants that are free from disease. Sow seeds as soon as they are ripe in summer or autumn, and keep the seedlings in a sheltered place to overwinter.

1 Preparing the seedbed
Fill a clean tray with moist seed-starting mix and firm it gently to about ½in (1cm) below the rim.

2 Sowing the seed
Use clean, folded paper to sow the seeds evenly and thinly over the surface.

3 Covering the seed
Cover with glass or clear plastic to retain moisture. Place in a cold frame until two pairs of leaves develop.

4 Pricking out
When plants are big enough to handle, transplant them into pots. Take care not to damage the stem or roots.

Dividing perennials

The most common way to increase perennials is by division. This eases overcrowding and—by removing weak and unproductive sections—also revitalizes older, less vigorous plants. Replant only healthy sections. Perennials are usually divided when dormant, in late autumn or early spring.

1 Lifting clumps
Water the plant before lifting. Then carefully insert a fork beyond the edge of the clump and lift gently to reduce the risk of root damage. Shake off excess soil.

2 Dividing by hand
Tease apart the roots by hand, keeping healthy sections. Cut back old or dead topgrowth. Dig new planting holes, water them, then replant the divisions.

Alternative methods

Dividing with back-to-back forks
For large, congested clumps of perennials, place two forks back to back, touching where the tines meet the shaft, and lever them apart to divide the root system.

Dividing with a spade
Use a sharp spade to chop through plants with tough, woody roots. For plants that won't divide easily, set the spade in position and stand on it with your full body weight.

A-Z of Perennials

Collect fully ripe seeds and sow them at 60°F (15°C). Seedlings take three years to flower. Protect plants from frost during their first winter.

A

Acanthus spinosus Bear's breeches

SHOWY, VERTICAL STEMS with white flowers protruding from purple bracts make this acanthus a striking accent plant. The ground-level leaves, which have spiny edges, are equally architectural and can grow up to 3ft (1m) long. Although tall, it is best sited toward the front of a border, with space around, so that both flowers and foliage can be seen clearly. Plant it in free-draining but rich soil, and take precautions against attacks from slugs and snails. The huge blooms can be dried for an indoor display, and the seed collected in the autumn for growing new plants.

OTHER VARIETIES *A. dioscoridis* var. *perringii* (shorter-growing, gray-green leaves); *A. hungaricus* (white or pale pink flowers); *A. mollis* (purple-tinted stems); *A. syriacus* (greenish white flowers).

PLANT PROFILE

HEIGHT 5ft (1.5m)

SPREAD 24in (60cm)

SITE Sun or partial shade

SOIL Fertile, free-draining

HARDINESS Z5–9 H9–5

FLOWERING Late spring to midsummer

Achillea filipendulina 'Gold Plate' Yarrow

FLAT HEADS OF GOLDEN FLOWERS on strong, erect stems produce a bold display throughout the summer, and combine well with crimson poppies, blue delphiniums, ox-eye daisies, and hollyhocks. The prolific flowers are good for cutting, lasting well in water without any special treatment, and they can also be dried for use in winter arrangements. Yarrow is easy to grow, tolerating a broad range of soil types. Although the stems are stiff, they tend to bend forward and may need some support. Note that the foliage can trigger skin allergies, and gloves should be worn when handling.

OTHER VARIETIES *A.* 'Lachsschönheit' (pink flowers); *A.* x *lewisii* 'King Edward' (low, mound-forming); *A.* 'Summerwine' (red flowers).

PLANT PROFILE
HEIGHT 4ft (1.2m)
SPREAD 18in (45cm)
SITE Full sun
SOIL Moist, free-draining
HARDINESS Z3–9 H9–1
FLOWERING Early summer to early autumn

A | *Aciphylla aurea* Bayonet plant

THIS UNUSUAL PERENNIAL FROM NEW ZEALAND may look far too exotic for cooler climates, but it is actually hardy in Zone 8. It makes a large clump of swordlike leaves, and the scores of tiny golden brown flowers (only appearing in long, hot summers) are protected by spiny growths. It needs to be grown in rich, free-draining soil with other architectural plants—if planted in the middle of a typical summer border, it can look out of place. The fruit is only produced when there are male and female plants in close proximity.

OTHER VARIETY *A. scott-thomsonii* (much taller-growing, yellowish green flowers).

PLANT PROFILE
HEIGHT 3ft (1m)
SPREAD 3ft (1m)
SITE Full sun
SOIL Fertile, free-draining
HARDINESS Z8–11 H12–8
FLOWERING Early to late summer

Aconitum carmichaelii 'Arendsii' Monkshood

A

STIFF, VERTICAL FLOWER STEMS with a profusion of deep violet or blue, hoodlike flowers held well clear of the dark green leaves make this a contender for cool-color-themed gardens. It also blends well with the white-flowering *Aconitum* x *cammarum* 'Grandiflorum Album'. Like all monkshoods, 'Arendsii' needs plenty of well-rotted organic matter forked into the soil, especially when grown in full sun, to keep the ground moist; semishade is best, however. Note that all parts of the monkshood are highly toxic if ingested, and contact with the skin can lead to an unpleasant irritation.

OTHER VARIETIES *A.* x *cammarum* 'Bicolor' (blue and white flowers); *A.* x *carmichaelii* 'Barker's Variety' (deep violet flowers).

PLANT PROFILE
HEIGHT To 4ft (1.2m)
SPREAD 12in (30cm)
SITE Partial shade or full sun
SOIL Moist, fertile
HARDINESS Z3–8 H8–3
FLOWERING Early autumn

A

Actaea rubra Red baneberry

FEATHERY, WHITE, EARLY-SUMMER FLOWERS and a profusion of tiny, bright red autumn berries are the big attractions. The best site is a lightly shaded garden where the soil is damp and enriched with plenty of leaf mold. Baneberry can also be grown on streambanks. If growing a couple of plants, include *Actaea alba* with its attractive white berries, each marked with a black spot. Plant all baneberries out of the reach of young children, since the berries are highly toxic if ingested. If you want young plants to fill out a display, divide clumps in early spring, before full growth begins.

OTHER VARIETIES *A. simplex* 'James Compton' (dark purple foliage, scented cream flowers); *A. spicata* (white flowers, black berries).

PLANT PROFILE

HEIGHT 18in (45cm)

SPREAD 12in (30cm)

SITE Partial shade

SOIL Moist, fertile

HARDINESS Z4–8 H8–1

FLOWERING Midspring to early summer

Adenophora bulleyana Gland bellflower

A

PLANT PROFILE

WITH FLOWERS LIKE THOSE OF A CAMPANULA that appear in clusters on top of tall, thin spikes, this plant is sometimes called the gland bellflower. Use it to inject late-summer color into the garden, to tower over shorter evergreen shrubs, or as part of the buildup to a tall focal point. It can be accommodated in borders where the soil is fertile and moist but free-draining, and can also be grown in wild gardens. Because mature plants dislike being moved, position yours carefully at the outset. In spring, as new growth emerges, look out for slugs and snails, which can cause serious damage.

OTHER VARIETIES *A. liliifolia* (shorter-growing, pale blue, fragrant flowers); *A. tashiroi* (branching stems, attractive foliage).

HEIGHT 4ft (1.2m)	
SPREAD 12in (30cm)	
SITE Sun or partial shade	
SOIL Moist, fertile, free-draining	
HARDINESS Z4–8 H8–1	
FLOWERING Late summer	

A | *Aegopodium podagraria* 'Variegatum' Variegated ground elder

THIS IS THE BEST AND ONLY type of ground elder to grow. It is extremely attractive but, although invasive, is not as thuggish as the parent plant, *Aegopodium podagraria*. 'Variegatum' has creamy white margins and markings on each leaf, and rather insignificant white flowers. It thrives in the shady parts of the garden and in any type of soil, including poor ground, making it excellent groundcover. Few ornamental plants can be grown on poor soil and in shade, and in these situations it does not pose a threat to other plants. When planting elsewhere, create a medium-size, walled planting hole, sealing the sides with old tiles or similar material, to help prevent the roots from spreading excessively.

PLANT PROFILE

HEIGHT 12–24in (30–60cm)

SPREAD Indefinite

SITE Full or partial shade

SOIL Average

HARDINESS Z4–9 H9–1

FLOWERING Early summer

DIVIDING CLUMPS

Dig up and divide large clumps in the spring. Using a clean, sharp knife, trim off all old stems and damaged tissue. Dust the wounds with fungicide to prevent rot, and replant the clumps in the garden.

Agapanthus 'Blue Giant' African lily

A

STARBURSTS OF RICH BLUE FLOWERS held above long sturdy stems make a bold statement in a midsummer border. This African lily also looks dramatic in large tubs positioned on patios, or when planted in groups in gravel gardens, especially when combined with *Agapanthus* 'Bressingham White' with its snow white blooms. Grow these plants in rich, free-draining soil, and make sure they have plenty of moisture during the growing season. Many agapanthus will not tolerate low temperatures, but this cultivar is hardier than most, especially when provided with a thick mulch of compost where winters are cold.

OTHER VARIETIES *A. campanulatus* (smaller-growing, grayish green leaves, sometimes white flowers); *A.* 'Loch Hope' (later-flowering).

PLANT PROFILE
HEIGHT 4ft (1.2m)
SPREAD 24in (60cm)
SITE Full sun
SOIL Moist, fertile, free-draining
HARDINESS Z7–10 H10–7
FLOWERING Mid- and late summer

A

Agastache foeniculum 'Alabaster' Anise hyssop

VERTICAL SPIKES OF WHITE FLOWERS make a pleasant backdrop to a pond in summer, although this plant will not enjoy the moist conditions at the water's edge, preferring free-draining soil. The aniseed-scented leaves are clumped beneath the flowers, offering shade and hiding places for frogs and toads. *Agastache foeniculum* needs protection in cold winters and must be planted in a sheltered spot—at the base of a warm wall is ideal—in reasonably fertile soil. Although this hyssop suffers from a reputation for being short-lived, this is not a problem because it self-seeds freely.

OTHER VARIETIES *A. barberi* (red-purple flowers); *A. barberi* 'Firebird' (copper flowers); *A. barberi* 'Tutti-Frutti' (dark pink-red flowers).

PLANT PROFILE
HEIGHT 3–5ft (1m–1.5m)
SPREAD 12in (30cm)
SITE Full sun
SOIL Fertile, free-draining
HARDINESS Z6-10
FLOWERING Midsummer to early autumn

Ajuga reptans 'Catlin's Giant' Bugle

A

THIS SPREADING EVERGREEN has tall, dark blue flower spikes, but its chief asset is the colorful dark bronze-purple foliage. It prefers moist soil, although this particular bugle is tolerant of a wide range of conditions, including poor ground and shade. Avoid deep shade, however, if you want the best foliage color. 'Multicolor', often sold as 'Rainbow', has equally attractive foliage with bronze-green leaves and unusual cream and pink markings. Of the bugles grown for their flowers, try *Ajuga reptans* 'Purple Torch', which has spikes of lavender-pink flowers. Divide plants in the spring or autumn.

OTHER VARIETIES *A. reptans* (dark green leaves); *A. reptans* 'Burgundy Glow' (silvery green leaves suffused with deep wine red); *A. reptans* 'Pink Elf' (compact with deep pink flowers).

PLANT PROFILE
HEIGHT 6in (15cm)
SPREAD 24–36in (60–90cm)
SITE Partial shade
SOIL Moist
HARDINESS Z3–9 H9–1
FLOWERING Late spring and early summer

A

Alchemilla mollis Lady's mantle

THIS INDISPENSABLE GROUNDCOVER PLANT self-seeds freely to form clumps of lime green leaves and sprays of tiny greenish yellow flowers, and is typically grown at the front edge of a border. To get the most out of it, shear the plant after its first flush of flowers to promote a second flowering and new leaves. Promptly removing dead flowers also prevents it from spreading. Lady's mantle thrives just about anywhere, even in poor soil, and is drought-tolerant. Use its foliage to contrast with, for example, purple or blue lavenders.

OTHER VARIETIES *A. alpina* (silver-hairy underside of leaves); *A. ellenbeckii* (smaller leaves and red stems); *A. xanthochlora* (yellow-green leaves, very free-flowering).

PLANT PROFILE
HEIGHT 24in (60cm)
SPREAD 30in (75cm)
SITE Sun or partial shade
SOIL Average
HARDINESS Z4–7 H7–1
FLOWERING Early summer to early autumn

Alopecurus pratensis 'Aureovariegatus' Foxtail grass

A

WITH ITS BRIGHT YELLOW AND GREEN STRIPES, 'Aureovariegatus' can be grown individually in a border or in drifts in wild gardens. The new foliage has a vibrant effect when grown in full sun, and is followed by tall thin stems with small reddish brown flowers that can be used in cut-flower displays, or left to stand over winter to add height and interest to the garden. To maintain the vigor of this grass when grown on heavy clay, clumps should be lifted and divided every few years, replanting only the younger outer sections. On poor soil, it may not grow to its full height.

OTHER VARIETY *A. pratensis* 'Aureus' (shorter grass, foliage with yellow margins and an inner green stripe).

PLANT PROFILE	
HEIGHT To 4ft (1.2m)	
SPREAD 16in (40cm)	
SITE Sun or partial shade	
SOIL Average	
HARDINESS Z5–8 H8–1	
FLOWERING Midspring to midsummer	

A

Alstroemeria ligtu hybrids Peruvian lily

THESE SHOWY, ATTRACTIVE EXOTICS will self-seed to form colorful clumps—from white to pink, yellow, and orange—at the front of a border. The only thing they lack is scent. New types keep appearing in garden nurseries that flower over a long summer period. Provide them with a sunny place in the border, as well as free-draining soil, since they dislike standing in cold, wet ground. Young plants should be covered with a thick mulch of compost in their first few winters.

OTHER VARIETIES *A. pygmaea* (smaller-growing, deep yellow flowers); *A. psittacina* (mauve-spotted stems, green flowers overlaid with red in summer).

PLANT PROFILE	
HEIGHT 20in (50cm)	
SPREAD 30in (75cm)	
SITE Full sun	
SOIL Free-draining	
HARDINESS Z8–11 H12–7	
FLOWERING Summer	

Amicia zygomeris

THIS HIGHLY UNUSUAL, DESIRABLE PERENNIAL has exceptionally straight, hollow stems, like thin bamboos, which fire up to well over head-height. The stems bear beautiful bright green leaves that from a distance look like large butterflies, their wings fully opened and flat. At the base of each leaf are small, flowerlike growths with purple veins. Grown mainly for its foliage, it produces pealike yellow flowers only in mild areas. It should be grown on free-draining, rich soil—against a warm, sunny, sheltered wall is ideal—and may need a protective winter mulch of compost. In cold areas, you can dig up the plant in the autumn, cut it back, and keep it in a pot in a frost-free place over the winter.

PLANT PROFILE

HEIGHT 7ft (2.2m)

SPREAD 4ft (1.2m)

SITE Full sun

SOIL Fertile, free-draining

HARDINESS Z8–10

FLOWERING Early and midautumn

A

Amsonia orientalis Blue star

THIS SLOW-GROWING PLANT, with its loose heads of small, violet-blue, star-shaped flowers, is ideal at the front of a bed or border. Sometimes known as blue star, amsonias are sun-loving and like free-draining soil, but they are by no means completely drought-tolerant. Their compact clumps are very attractive when planted at the foot of shrub roses, hiding the base of their bare stems. Amsonias can be divided in the spring if more plants are required, and they are usually very reliable, rarely falling victim to pests or diseases.

OTHER VARIETIES *A. illustris* (taller-growing, light blue flowers); *A. tabernaemontana* (lance-shaped leaves, free-flowering); *A. tabernaemontana* var. *salicifolia* (narrow leaves, flowerheads more open).

PLANT PROFILE
HEIGHT 20in (50cm)
SPREAD 12in (30cm)
SITE Full sun
SOIL Free-draining
HARDINESS Z5–8 H8–5
FLOWERING Early and midsummer

Anaphalis triplinervis Pearl everlasting

A

ATTRACTIVE WHITE FLOWERS are not the only reason for growing this plant—its gray green, white-woolly leaves have even greater appeal. Like most silver-leaved plants, it likes a hot site in the garden and good drainage, but if the soil dries out too much, the stems will quickly start to wilt. It is also possible to grow it in slightly shaded, moist ground. Plant it either as part of a white color scheme, or to offset contrasting rich blues and reds. The stems can also be cut and used fresh or dried for indoor flower displays, where they will look particularly effective within a green foliage arrangement.

OTHER VARIETIES *A. margaritacea* (smaller-growing); *A. triplinervis* 'Sommerschnee' (brilliant white bracts).

PLANT PROFILE

HEIGHT 32–36in (80–90cm)

SPREAD 18–24in (45–60cm)

SITE Full sun

SOIL Free-draining

HARDINESS Z3–8 H8–1

FLOWERING Mid- and late summer

A *Anchusa azurea* 'Loddon Royalist' Italian bugloss

THE EXCEPTIONAL, ROYAL BLUE FLOWERS of this plant are highly useful at the start of summer. Strong, erect stems hold up the flower spikes, which look beautiful among aquilegias or with a yellow-stemmed bamboo behind. After the first flush of blooms, cut back the stems to encourage a second flowering. The key to success is free-draining, fertile soil—if the plant sits in wet soil, it will quickly rot. It is short-lived, so take root cuttings or replace every few years, since young plants give a better show of flowers. The similar, though smaller, *Anchusa cespitosa* looks good in a rock garden.

OTHER VARIETIES *A. azurea* 'Feltham Pride' (compact, clear blue flowers); *A. azurea* 'Little John' (dwarf, long-lived, deep blue flowers).

PLANT PROFILE		
HEIGHT 3ft (1m)		
SPREAD 24in (60cm)		
SITE Full sun		
SOIL Fertile, free-draining		
HARDINESS Z3–8 H8–1		
FLOWERING Early summer		

Anemone nemorosa 'Robinsoniana' Windflower

A

FOR PALE LAVENDER-BLUE FLOWERS, each with a creamy gray back, 'Robinsoniana' is the form of windflower to choose. It likes rich, moist soil, but will tolerate drier conditions when dormant in the summer. Other good forms of the windflower include 'Flore Pleno', with its white double flowers, and 'Wilk's Giant', which has the largest flowers in this group. Grow windflowers in groups among bright yellow buttercups and pale yellow primroses for a highly effective carpet of spring color.

OTHER VARIETIES *A. nemorosa* (vigorous, white, pink-flushed flowers); *A. nemorosa* 'Allenii' (deep lavender-blue flowers); *A. nemorosa* 'Bowles' Purple' (rich purple flowers).

PLANT PROFILE
HEIGHT 3–6in (8–15cm)
SPREAD 12in (30cm)
SITE Partial shade
SOIL Moist, fertile
HARDINESS Z4–8 H8–1
FLOWERING Spring to early summer

A

Anemone x *hybrida* 'Königin Charlotte' Japanese anemone

FOR BEAUTIFUL COLORS, good height, and open, cheerful flowers, the Japanese anemone is indispensable for the late summer/autumn garden. 'Königin Charlotte' (also called 'Queen Charlotte') has large double pink flowers and, like most Japanese anemones, soon forms a big clump. It prefers rich, moist soil, but dislikes heavy, wet ground over winter. Plant these tall perennials in borders, beside ornamental grasses, with late-flowering clematis and annual cosmos, and in front of *Hydrangea aspera* subsp. *sargentiana*. In long, dry summers, water the roots well and then add a thick mulch of compost.

OTHER VARIETIES   *A.* x *hybrida* 'Elegans' (single, pale pink flowers);
A. x *hybrida* 'Honorine Jobert' (white flowers with a yellow eye).

PLANT PROFILE
HEIGHT 4–5ft (1.2–1.5m)
SPREAD Indefinite
SITE Full sun or partial shade
SOIL Moist, fertile
HARDINESS Z4–8 H8–5
FLOWERING Late summer to midautumn

Anemonopsis macrophylla False anemone

FOR WILD OR WOODLAND AREAS, or any shady part of the garden, this is an excellent plant to choose. It has attractive, 3in- (8cm-) long leaves, and black wiry flower stems that shoot up through the foliage. From a distance, the small, scattered, cup-shaped, nodding flowers resemble hovering insects. The soil must be acidic, moist, and on the rich side, and some protection from penetrating cold winds is important to prevent the foliage from suffering badly. A native of the mountainous woodland areas of Japan, it could also be used as a fringe plant for an ornamental Asian-style garden.

PLANT PROFILE

HEIGHT 30in (75cm)

SPREAD 18in (45cm)

SITE Partial shade

SOIL Acidic, moist, fertile

HARDINESS Z5–8 H8–5

FLOWERING Mid- and late summer

A

Angelica gigas Korean angelica

TALL, THIN, PURPLE-FLOWERING STEMS high above the dramatic large leaves inject color into the edge of a wooded area or wild garden. A large plant that self-seeds prolifically in moist, fertile soil, it also suits a site close to a riverbank or the edge of a natural pond, where its leafy growth provides cover and shade for frogs and toads. Although new shoots can be devoured by slugs and snails, these pests will not make much impact on a massed spread of plants. Angelica is a short-lived plant, but watch for self-sown seedlings near the parent and move them to a preferred position before they grow too large.

OTHER VARIETY *A. archangelica* (greenish yellow flowers).

PLANT PROFILE

HEIGHT 3–6ft (1–2m)

SPREAD 4ft (1.2m)

SITE Full sun

SOIL Moist, fertile

HARDINESS Z4–9 H8–2

FLOWERING Late summer and early autumn

Anthemis tinctoria 'E.C. Buxton' Golden marguerite

A

PALE LEMON YELLOW FLOWERS, with a slightly darker eye, add a bright and breezy note to the early summer garden and are an asset to cottage gardens and borders before the midsummer planting plan comes into its own. The one problem is that plants are short-lived, although they can be easily propagated by dividing clumps in the spring or late summer; alternatively, early summer cuttings quickly take root. Deadheading should provide a second flush of flowers, though not quite as impressive as the first. There are many excellent alternatives for a big border.

OTHER VARIETIES *A. tinctoria* 'Kelwayi' (clear, mid-yellow flowers); *A. tinctoria* 'Sauce Hollandaise' (cream, almost white, flowers).

PLANT PROFILE	
HEIGHT	3ft (1m)
SPREAD	3ft (1m)
SITE	Full sun
SOIL	Free-draining
HARDINESS	Z3–8 H8–3
FLOWERING	Summer

A | *Anthriscus sylvestris* 'Ravenswing' Cow parsley

THIS EASILY OVERLOOKED, SHORT-LIVED PLANT has a superb open
structure of stems topped by white flowers above purple-brown
leaves. It is an essential component in a cottage or wild garden—
even in formal gardens, it adds a light and airy touch before the
main plants start performing. It can also be grown as a biennial, but
the easiest way to raise new plants is to look for seedlings scattered
around the parent and transplant them to a preferred position.
Don't cut off the flower heads too early or the seed will not have
a chance to ripen and scatter. Alternatively, you can collect the seed
from the flowers and sow it in the autumn in pots of seed-starting
mix. Keep the seedlings outside in a sheltered position.

PLANT PROFILE

HEIGHT 3ft (1m)

SPREAD 12in (30cm)

SITE Sun or partial shade

SOIL Free-draining

HARDINESS Z7–10

FLOWERING Midspring to
early summer

Aquilegia vulgaris var. *stellata* 'Nora Barlow' Granny's bonnet

A

A QUINTESSENTIAL COTTAGE GARDEN PLANT, 'Nora Barlow' has downward-pointing pompons of pink and cream petals, unlike typical aquilegias with their open funnels. 'Nora Barlow' self-seeds freely around the garden and is happy in a wide range of situations and soils. The pastel flowers combine well with the royal blue *Anchusa azurea* 'Loddon Royalist', or grow it as part of a collection of aquilegias, which should also include the North American State and Songbird Series with their excellent colors and long spurs.

OTHER VARIETIES *A. caerulea* (blue and white flowers with slender spurs); *A. flabellata* (soft blue–purple flowers with white petal tips); *A.* Mckana Hybrids (vigorous, short-lived, in shades of blue, yellow, and red).

PLANT PROFILE
HEIGHT 3ft (1m)
SPREAD 18in (45cm)
SITE Full sun or partial shade
SOIL Moist, free-draining
HARDINESS Z4–7 H7–1
FLOWERING Late spring and early summer

A | *Arisaema candidissimum* Striped cobra lily

WONDERFULLY WEIRD AND SHAPELY, this is a deceptively easy plant to grow when given rich, neutral to slightly acidic, moist soil and light shade among deciduous shrubs. *Arisaema candidissimum* sends up a quirky pink and white spathe (modified leaf), like a vertical funnel, with prominent lips and a protruding short point over the top that hides the real flowers deep inside it. Growth is not visible until early summer, and the leaf (there is only one) can grow up to 8in (20cm) long. It is best given a protective mulch of compost when the temperature dives during winter.

OTHER VARIETIES *A. amurense* (purple spathes with white stripes); *A. flavum* (small yellow spathes); *A. tortuosum* (hooded green spathes).

PLANT PROFILE

HEIGHT 16in (40cm)

SPREAD 6in (15cm)

SITE Partial shade

SOIL Moist, fertile

HARDINESS Z7–9 H9–7

FLOWERING Summer

Arisarum proboscideum Mouse plant

A

THE DARK BROWN-PURPLE FLOWERS, which are actually modified leaves known as spathes, look like tiny animals with long, whippy tails, and give rise to this plant's common name. These "flowers" are tucked up among, and are often obscured by, the bases of the thin leaves, and in order to see them clearly it is important to place the mouse plant where it can be seen easily. Provide moist, rich soil and woodland-type conditions and it will spread to form large colonies. The tubers should be planted in autumn, at which time established clumps can also be divided. To do this, dig up a small patch, then carefully separate the tubers and replant healthy individual sections in similar growing conditions.

PLANT PROFILE
HEIGHT 6in (15cm)
SPREAD To 10in (25cm)
SITE Partial shade
SOIL Moist, fertile
HARDINESS Z7–9 H9–1
FLOWERING Spring

A

Armeria maritima 'Alba' Sea thrift

GROWING IN GRASSY LITTLE MOUNDS, this plant colonizes clifftops and seashores. The dark green, stiff, spiky leaves bristle on the ground and are topped by 8in- (20cm-) high flower stems, each with a rounded flowerhead. Sea thrift is easy to grow and likes poor to moderately fertile, free-draining soil—it will not be happy in moist or fertile conditions. It can be grown in rock gardens, as an edging plant, or even on the top of a stone wall. Divide established clumps in the spring and replant the outer sections.

OTHER VARIETIES *A. maritima* (profusely borne white, pink, or red-purple flowers); *A. maritima* 'Bloodstone' (dark red flowers); *A. maritima* 'Vindictive' (rose pink flowers).

PLANT PROFILE

HEIGHT 8in (20cm)

SPREAD 12in (30cm)

SITE Full sun

SOIL Average, free-draining

HARDINESS Z4–8

FLOWERING Late spring to summer

Artemisia ludoviciana 'Silver Queen' Western mugwort

A

THE SILVERY WHITE LEAVES are the main feature of this plant, rather than the plumes of brown-yellow flowers, which some people remove before they open. 'Silver Queen' is at the top of any list for a white garden. To keep it compact and encourage the attractive young leaves, prune it in spring. It can also be cut to the ground in the autumn and covered with a protective dry mulch during the winter. It does best in free-draining, fertile soil—in moist conditions it may not survive many years. *Artemisia absinthium* 'Lambrook Silver' is a superb alternative and also grows up to 30in (75cm) high.

OTHER VARIETIES *A. glacialis* (lower-growing); *A. lactiflora* (creamy white flowers); *A. schmidtiana* (small yellow flowers).

PLANT PROFILE
HEIGHT 30in (75cm)
SPREAD 24in (60cm)
SITE Full sun
SOIL Fertile, free-draining
HARDINESS Z5–11 H12–8
FLOWERING Midsummer to autumn

A *Arum italicum* 'Marmoratum' Lords and ladies

WONDERFULLY PATTERNED, MARBLED LEAVES from winter to late spring, and a startling vertical yellow flower, make this a superb plant for a sheltered site. Even better, the flower is followed by bright orange-red berries that last until the end of summer. During its dormant summer period it likes to be on the dry side, after which new leaves start emerging in midautumn. Mulch with compost in winter and spring after heavy rain to keep moisture in the ground. Remove the mulch in summer. Note that the sap and juice of the berries can cause skin irritation, and the berries are toxic if ingested.

OTHER VARIETIES *A. creticum* (dark green, unmarked leaves); *A. pictum* (smaller-growing, blackish purple spathes).

PLANT PROFILE

HEIGHT 12in (30cm)

SPREAD 6in (15cm)

SITE Sun or partial shade

SOIL Fertile, free-draining

HARDINESS Z7–9 H9–3

FLOWERING Early summer

Aruncus dioicus 'Kneiffi' Goat's beard

A

THIS IS A TALL, HIGH-IMPACT PLANT for the back of the border, featuring large sprays of tiny flowers held well clear of lacy, deeply divided leaves. Totally undemanding, it can be grown in most positions but thrives in shade and moist, rich soil—for example, by a stream or natural pond. 'Kneiffi' quickly self-seeds and spreads, so if you don't want any more plants, you must cut off the flowerheads as soon as they start to fade. The male creamy white flowers and female greenish white blooms are found on the same plant and make excellent cut flowers for flamboyant, architectural displays.

OTHER VARIETIES *A. aethusifolius* (shorter); *A. dioicus* (taller).

PLANT PROFILE
HEIGHT To 6ft (2m)
SPREAD 4ft (1.2m)
SITE Full or partial shade
SOIL Moist, fertile
HARDINESS Z3–7 H7–1
FLOWERING Early and midsummer

Arundo donax var. *versicolor* Giant reed

SIMILAR TO A BAMBOO IN LOOKS and habit, this plant throws up impressive, sturdy stems with white-striped leaves that can grow up to 24in (60cm) long. Its green to purple flowers are unlikely to develop in temperate gardens, even in good conditions and rich, moist soil, but this doesn't matter because it makes a superb foliage plant or summer screen, especially in a Japanese-style garden. Cut it back to the ground in the first half of winter to guarantee attractive fresh leaves the following spring. The parent of this variety, *Arundo donax* (giant reed), is the tallest hardy grass, growing up to 5m (15ft) high, and rarely needs staking.

OTHER VARIETY *A. donax* (mid-green leaves).

PLANT PROFILE
HEIGHT To 6ft (2m)
SPREAD 24in (60cm)
SITE Full sun
SOIL Moist, fertile
HARDINESS Z7–15 H12–1
FLOWERING Mid- and late autumn

NEW PLANTS

Seeds collected in autumn, when the berries dry and split, can be sown in the spring at 50°F (10°C); or, in late autumn, tease apart the rhizomes, retaining a few growing points on each, and plant out.

Asphodeline lutea King's spear

A

EMERGING FROM LONG, SLENDER, BLUE–GREEN grassy foliage, these extraordinary plants send up erect spikes topped with open, starlike flowers. The straw yellow, gently scented blooms are followed by impressive green berries. Grow it in a Mediterranean-style garden or at the base of a sunny wall in fertile, well-drained (but not arid) soil. If you want even more plants, they are easily propagated by seed, or by digging up the bulb-like rhizome and dividing it in late summer. In colder areas, young plants will need a thick mulch of compost during their first couple of winters.

OTHER VARIETY *A. liburnica* (midsummer-flowering).

PLANT PROFILE	
HEIGHT	3ft (1m)
SPREAD	12in (30cm)
SITE	Full sun
SOIL	Fertile, Free-draining
HARDINESS	Z6–9 H9–6
FLOWERING	Late spring

Asphodelus albus Asphodel

THIS COTTAGE GARDEN PLANT has erect stems, reaching 3ft (1m)
high, covered with open white flowers right up to the top. Asphodel
is a useful gap filler in the garden, requiring only free-draining
soil and bright sun to look its best; if it is being grown in rich soil,
however, it will grow even taller and will need staking to keep it
erect. Grow it with tall alliums or an underplanting of red tulips for
a dramatic effect. *Asphodelus fistulosus*, which has beautiful, small star-
shaped flowers with a red line running up to the point of each
petal, is a good alternative but more difficult to find.

PLANT PROFILE

HEIGHT 3ft (1m)

SPREAD 12in (30cm)

SITE Sun

SOIL Average, free-draining

HARDINESS Z7–11 H12–7

FLOWERING Mid- or late
spring

Astelia chathamica Silver spear

A

THIS PUNCHY, DRAMATIC EVERGREEN from New Zealand has sword-shaped, silvery blue leaves that grow up to 4ft (1.2m) long. The yellowish green flowers are insignificant. It needs moist, acidic soil that should not be allowed to dry out, especially in summer, when you must water it well during prolonged dry spells. In addition, water it in spring and then add a thick mulch of compost to help keep moisture in the ground through the growing season. It will usually regrow in the spring if it is cut back by winter frost. Use it as a feature plant, where no other plants will compete with it and ruin the effect.

OTHER VARIETY *A. nervosa* (hardier, smaller-growing).

PLANT PROFILE
HEIGHT 4ft (1.2m)
SPREAD To 6ft (2m)
SITE Sun or partial shade
SOIL Acidic, moist, fertile
HARDINESS Z8–15 H12–10
FLOWERING Mid- and late spring

A | *Aster novae-angliae* 'Purple Dome' New England aster

BLOOMING PROFUSELY right at the end of the season, injecting bright shades of pink, lilac, purple *(see inset)*, and white, asters are well worth their place in any border. Many grow up to 5ft (1.5m) high, but 'Purple Dome' is nicely compact. Divide it every three years to keep it vigorous, or take cuttings in spring. Like all New England asters, it prefers rich, moist soil and tolerates some shade. Unlike New York asters *(Aster novi-belgii)*, New England asters do not have a problem with mildew.

OTHER VARIETIES *A. novae-angliae* 'Andenken an Alma Pötschke' (salmon pink flowers); *A. novae-angliae* 'Harrington's Pink' (light pink flowers); *A. novi-belgii* 'Kristina' large, (semidouble, white flowers).

PLANT PROFILE
HEIGHT 24in (60cm)
SPREAD 24in (60cm)
SITE Sun or partial shade
SOIL Moist, fertile
HARDINESS Z3–9 H9–1
FLOWERING Late summer to midautumn

Aster pilosus var. *pringlei* 'Monte Cassino' Frost aster

A

COVERED BY PROLIFIC SPRAYS of white daisylike flowers, each with a yellow eye, this plant needs moist, rich soil to promote plenty of blooms, although it will not tolerate waterlogged conditions in the winter. If the ground is too wet, dig up the plant, keep it in a cool greenhouse, and plant it out the following spring. Alternatively, since 'Monte Cassino' flowers best in its first year, take cuttings in the spring and discard the parent after it has flowered. Plant the cuttings out 12 months later. The flower sprays make excellent cut flowers.

OTHER VARIETIES *A. alpinus* (smaller-growing, violet flowers); *A. amellus* 'Veilchenkönigin' (violet-purple flowers); 'Coombe Fishacre' (pink-flushed white flowers); *A. turbinellus* (pale violet flowers).

PLANT PROFILE
HEIGHT To 3ft (1m)
SPREAD 12in (30cm)
SITE Sun or partial shade
SOIL Moist but free-draining, fertile
HARDINESS Z4–8
FLOWERING Late summer to midautumn

A

Astilbe x *arendsii* 'Fanal'

WITH ERECT, FLUFFY PLUMES of tiny, dark crimson flowers above the 9in- (23cm-) long leaves, 'Fanal' adds rich tones to a bog garden or very damp part of a border. Like all astilbes, it needs a permanently moist, fertile soil, with well-rotted compost added to it every year. Although flowering is restricted to early summer, the panicles gradually turn brown and continue into winter without looking ragged or tired. 'Fanal' makes an excellent backdrop to a wide range of moisture-loving plants from *Iris ensata* (Japanese flag) to *Ligularia*.

OTHER VARIETIES *A.* x *arendsii* 'Brautschleier' (white flowers); *A.* x *arendsii* 'Irrlicht' (white flowers, dark green leaves); *A.* x *crispa* 'Perkeo' (compact, deep pink flowers); 'Sprite' (shell pink flowers).

PLANT PROFILE	
HEIGHT 24in (60cm)	
SPREAD 18in (45cm)	
SITE Full sun	
SOIL Moist, fertile	
HARDINESS Z3–8 H8–2	
FLOWERING Early summer	

Astilboides tabularis Shieldleaf Rodgers flower

IF YOU WANT A WATERSIDE PLANT with big, bold foliage but don't have room for the very large and dominating *Gunnera manicata*, you can grow this Chinese perennial instead. Individual leaves are about 3ft (1m) long, and held on tall stems up to 4ft (1.2m) high, while the creamy white flowers give the plant an extra 12in (30cm) of height in early and midsummer. The rounded leaves are lobed and toothed, making them even more dramatic, and they create the perfect shaded canopy for frogs to hide beneath. This plant needs to be grown in light shade on damp soil that never dries out.

PLANT PROFILE

HEIGHT 5ft (1.5m)

SPREAD 4ft (1.2m)

SITE Partial shade

SOIL Moist

HARDINESS Z5–7 H7–4

FLOWERING Early and midsummer

Astrantia major 'Hadspen Blood' Masterwort

THIS WONDERFUL VARIETY really stands out in a cottage garden. All types of masterwort have pincushion flowers on wiry stems and, as its name suggests, the blooms of 'Hadspen Blood' are dark red. It needs a sunny position to bring out its colors, unlike most other astrantias, which thrive in shade. It also requires rich, moist soil to do well. Grow it with the white *Astrantia major* for contrast. Other red astrantias include 'Ruby Wedding' and 'Rubra', while *A. major* var. *rosea* has pink tints. Propagate 'Hadspen Blood' by division in spring; each section needs a growing point and its own root system.

OTHER VARIETIES *A. major* subsp. 'Shaggy' (long bracts with green tips); *A. major* 'Sunningdale Variegated' (leaves with creamy margins).

PLANT PROFILE
HEIGHT 3ft (1m)
SPREAD 18in (45cm)
SITE Full sun
SOIL Moist, fertile
HARDINESS Z4–7 H7–1
FLOWERING Early and midsummer

Baptisia australis False indigo

B

PRODUCING A GOOD SHOW of dark blue, pealike flowers on erect stems held clear of the leaves, this plant really comes to life in early summer. Even when the flowers fade, the foliage gives a vigorous, fresh, bright look for the rest of the season. Its long roots need deep, rich, moist but well–drained soil, although it grows on sandy soil in the wild and will, therefore, also tolerate drier ground. Make sure you choose the right position from the beginning, because once in the ground and well established, the deep roots dislike being disturbed.

PLANT PROFILE
HEIGHT 5ft (1.5m)
SPREAD 24in (60cm)
SITE Full sun
SOIL Fertile, moist but free-draining
HARDINESS Z3–9 H9–1
FLOWERING Early summer

B

Belamcanda chinensis Blackberry lily

AN INTRIGUING PLANT that needs to be the center of attention in its own display, where it is not overshadowed by bolder, brasher plants. Its short, swordlike leaves grow straight out of the ground (like those of an iris), while the tall, slim stems carry starlike, yellow to orange-red flowers covered with maroon spots (*see inset*). There is a quick succession of flowers, each lasting only one day, and the blooms are followed by capsules containing large black seeds. Provide it with a thick winter mulch of compost or grow it in a sunny, sheltered site. Propagate by dividing plants in the spring, or by carefully forking young seedlings out of the ground and moving them to a prepared position in the garden.

PLANT PROFILE

HEIGHT 18–36in (45–90cm)

SPREAD 8in (20cm)

SITE Full sun or partial shade

SOIL Moist, fertile, free-draining

HARDINESS Z5–9 H9–5

FLOWERING Summer

EASY DIVISION

After flowering, gently pull large clumps into smaller sections, each with a root system and healthy buds, ready for replanting where needed.

Bergenia 'Bressingham White' Elephant's ears

B

THIS FIRST-RATE FRONT-OF-BORDER PLANT has large leaves with clear white flowers on short, strong stems. It makes a good backdrop to a pond, where it should be planted in free-draining soil away from the water's edge, or to soften the straight edges of bordering paths. Other bergenias have leaves that redden up in the winter—the deep pink 'Eric Smith' being one of the best—and where plants are chosen for their leaf color, an exposed site with poor soil is best; in other cases, plant in more fertile ground.

OTHER VARIETIES *B.* 'Ballawley' (bronze-purple winter foliage); *B. cordifolia* 'Purpurea' (magenta flowers, red leaves); *B.* 'Morgenröte' (reddish pink flowers); *B. purpurascens* (beet red winter foliage).

PLANT PROFILE

HEIGHT 12–18in (30–45cm)

SPREAD 18–24in (45–60cm)

SITE Sun or partial shade

SOIL Free-draining

HARDINESS Z4–9 H9–2

FLOWERING Mid- and late spring

B

Bouteloua gracilis Blue grama

WHILE MOST GRASSES MAKE BIG CLUMPS, this is a gem of a short grass from the dry plains of southern North America. The brush-like, brownish purple flowers stick out horizontally, and initially have a red hue before turning beige. Blue grama makes excellent fringe planting on the sunny side of an island bed, to the front of a border, and in gravel. It can be planted in geometric patterns—for example, in alternating squares—and can even be mowed where large clumps have formed. You need only buy a few plants because they self-seed quickly when grown in light, free-draining soil.

OTHER VARIETY *B. curtipendula* (taller, with smaller flowerheads).

PLANT PROFILE
HEIGHT To 20in (50cm)
SPREAD 12in (30cm)
SITE Full sun
SOIL Free-draining
HARDINESS Z5–9 H9–5
FLOWERING Summer

Boykinia aconitifolia Brook saxifrage

THIS MODEST, RELIABLE PERENNIAL is suitable for a half-shady site with moist, rich, acidic soil. It produces sprays of white, bell-shaped flowers with a yellow-tinged center, and attractive, rounded, deeply lobed leaves. Grow it in a wild or wooded area of the garden, or at the shady end of a border. Extra plants can be produced by dividing a clump in the spring and replanting the sections wherever they are needed in the garden.

OTHER VARIETY *Boykinia jamesii* (much shorter plant, with pinkish red flowers).

PLANT PROFILE

HEIGHT 6–24in (15–60cm)

SPREAD 12in (30cm)

SITE Partial shade

SOIL Acidic, moist, fertile

HARDINESS Z5–9 H9–5

FLOWERING Early and midsummer

B

Briza media Common quaking grass

THIS SHORT, LIGHT, AIRY GRASS makes a clump of fresh green leaves topped by stems with dangling, oatlike flowerheads. Initially the flowers are tinged red, but they gradually fade to beige. Quaking grass adds a fun touch when grown on the sunny side of fruit trees or in rock gardens, and is excellent for use in cut or dried flower displays. *Briza media* is easy to grow, and is adaptable to most soils, including light and heavy types. Large clumps can be divided in spring, and the old growth can be cut back in midsummer to promote fresh new leaves, although you will lose the attractive straw-colored seedheads in the process.

OTHER VARIETY *B. maxima* (shorter, leaves edged with pale green).

PLANT PROFILE

HEIGHT 24–36in (60–90cm)

SPREAD 12in (30cm)

SITE Full sun

SOIL Moist

HARDINESS Z4–11 H12–1

FLOWERING Late spring to midsummer

Brunnera macrophylla Siberian bugloss

THIS FLOWERING GROUNDCOVER PLANT has sprays of bright blue flowers, like forget-me-nots, among heart-shaped leaves. It is not so invasive that it ever becomes a major problem, and you can easily slice down through the roots with a spade and dig out any excess growth. It prefers light shade where the soil is moist, but if grown in a sunnier, more open position, mulch it well with compost after heavy rain to lock moisture in the ground. 'Hadspen Cream' has white markings on the leaf edges, as does the attractive 'Dawson's White'; both of these variegated varieties are best grown in shadier positions in the garden.

OTHER VARIETY *B. macrophylla* 'Betty Bowring' (white flowers).

PLANT PROFILE	
HEIGHT 18in (45cm)	
SPREAD 24in (60cm)	
SITE Light shade	
SOIL Moist	
HARDINESS Z3–7 H7–1	
FLOWERING Mid- and late spring	

C

Calamagrostis x *acutiflora* 'Karl Foerster' Feather reed grass

THIS BEAUTIFUL GRASS FORMS A CLUMP of wonderful arching leaves from spring to winter. In summer, the ramrod-erect flowering stems that shoot up from the center hold feathery red-tinged panicles that fade to beige and catch the breeze. Use 'Karl Foerster' in a gravel garden, or as a focal point in a border with low plants in front, to allow it to be fully appreciated. It prefers free-draining fertile soil, but will still perform well in clay. Leave the flowering stems through winter to provide shape in the garden, but cut them back in early spring before the new growth appears.

OTHER VARIETY C. 'Overdam' (lower-growing, leaves with pale yellow margins and stripes).

PLANT PROFILE
HEIGHT To 6ft (2m)
SPREAD 24in (60cm)
SITE Sun or partial shade
SOIL Fertile, free-draining
HARDINESS Z5–9 H9–4
FLOWERING Mid- and late summer

Calamintha nepeta Lesser calamint

C

PLANT PROFILE

HEIGHT To 18in (45cm)

SPREAD 20–30in (50–75cm)

SITE Sun or partial shade

SOIL Free-draining

HARDINESS Z6–11 H10–1

FLOWERING Late summer

A GOOD CHOICE FOR GRAVEL GARDENS, lesser calamint flowers in the second half of summer when many other garden plants lack color. The mauve, sometimes pink, flowers attract butterflies and bees, and the leaves are scented. It grows wild in central France and the Pyrenees, and bright sun and free-draining soil are essential; it will not tolerate ground that stays cold and wet. The dark pink *Calamintha grandiflora*, which grows to the same height, is slightly bushier and prefers light, dappled shade.

OTHER VARIETIES *C. grandiflora* 'Variegata' (aromatic, green and cream variegated leaves); *C. nepeta* subsp. *nepeta* 'White Cloud' (white flowers in spring and summer).

C | *Caltha palustris* Kingcup

AN IDEAL PLANT FOR A BOG GARDEN or wet ground at the edge of a pond, where you can enjoy its flashy yellow blooms in the spring. The flowers are offset by the dark leaves and the brown, muddy ground. It is possible to grow kingcup in a border if you make sure the soil is constantly wet. If you have the space for more than one plant, grow 'Flore Pleno', which has double yellow flowers. *Caltha palustris* var. *palustris* (giant marsh marigold) is the biggest and showiest of the kingcups, with flowers 3in (8cm) wide.

OTHER VARIETIES *C. palustris* var. *alba* (compact-growing, white flowers); *C. leptosepala* (silvery white flowers on leafless stems).

PLANT PROFILE
HEIGHT 4–16in (10–40cm)
SPREAD 18in (45cm)
SITE Full sun
SOIL Wet
HARDINESS Z3–7 H7–1
FLOWERING Spring

Campanula garganica 'Dickson's Gold' Adriatic bellflower

THIS TINY BEAUTY OF A CAMPANULA can be grown in pots, wall crevices, or rock gardens. Although small, it is robust and thrives in moist but free-draining soil. Other good, short campanulas include the rich purple, self-seeding *Campanula poscharskyana*, which is 6in (15cm) high, spreading to 20in (50cm), and the creamy white *C. poscharskyana* 'E.H. Frost'. The deep purple *C. portenschlagiana* also reaches a height of 6in (15cm), and is similarly grown to soften path edges or to spread across the top and sides of a stone wall.

OTHER VARIETIES (all short) *C. carpatica* (large, solitary, bell-shaped, blue, purple, or white flowers); *C. carpatica* 'Weisse Clips' (abundant white flowers).

PLANT PROFILE
HEIGHT 2in (5cm)
SPREAD 12in (30cm)
SITE Sun or partial shade
SOIL Moist but free-draining
HARDINESS Z4–7 H7–1
FLOWERING Summer

C | *Campanula takesimana* 'Elizabeth' Korean bellflower

THE REDDISH PURPLE-TINGED FLOWERS with maroon speckling within are so attractive that it's easy to ignore the plant's tendency to spread. If it does get out of hand, simply slice the roots with a spade and dig out the excess growth. The stems will need some support—twiggy sticks pushed into the soil as new growth appears in spring are ideal. Combine 'Elizabeth' with other medium-sized campanulas, such as *Campanula glomerata* (clustered bellflower), with its violet-to-lavender or white flowers. Both need moist but free-draining soil.

OTHER VARIETIES (all medium) *C. alliariifolia* (tubular to bell-shaped white flowers); *C.* 'Burghaltii' (grayish lavender-blue flowers); *C. sarmatica* (hairy light gray-blue flowers).

PLANT PROFILE

HEIGHT 14–16in (35–40cm)

SPREAD 16in (40cm)

SITE Sun or partial shade

SOIL Moist but free-draining

HARDINESS Z5–8

FLOWERING Summer

Campanula trachelium 'Bernice' Nettle-leaved bellflower

C

ALTHOUGH NOT THE VERY TALLEST CAMPANULA, 'Bernice' still needs staking to keep it upright. Its beautiful double lilac-blue flowers are perfect for the middle of a border in a cottage-style garden, and it mixes well with the white 'Alba Flore Pleno', which also has double flowers. There are several other first-rate tall campanulas that will combine well with 'Bernice'. These include the white to pale blue *Campanula lactiflora* (milky bellflower), 4–5ft (1.2–1.5m) high and the lilac-pink *C. lactiflora* 'Loddon Anna'.

OTHER VARIETIES (all tall) *C. lactiflora* 'Alba' (pure white flowers); *C. latifolia* 'Brantwood' (deep violet flowers); *C. latiloba* 'Percy Piper' (rich lavender-blue flowers).

PLANT PROFILE		
HEIGHT 18–36in (45–90cm)		
SPREAD 12in (30cm)		
SITE Sun or partial shade		
SOIL Moist but free-draining		
HARDINESS Z5–8 H8–5		
FLOWERING Summer		

C

Cardamine pratensis 'Flore Pleno' Cuckoo flower

DOUBLE FLOWERS ON STIFF, ERECT STEMS, held well above the glossy dark green foliage, create a lilac-pink show in shady borders or wooded areas of the garden. Many of the cardamines are weeds, but the compact, clump-forming 'Flore Pleno' is well worth growing—as is 'Edith', which has double white flowers opening from pink buds. All cardamines like rich, moist soil, except the smaller white-flowering *Cardamine trifolia*, which prefers free-draining conditions.

OTHER VARIETIES *C. pentaphylla* (clump-forming with white, purple, or lilac flowers); *C. pratensis* (gray-green to glossy dark green leaves); *C. raphanifolia* (taller-growing).

PLANT PROFILE
HEIGHT 12–18in (30–45cm)
SPREAD 12in (30cm)
SITE Full or partial shade
SOIL Moist, fertile
HARDINESS Z5–8 H8–5
FLOWERING Late spring

Carex flagellifera Sedge

C

THE TALL, ARCHING THIN LEAVES of this New Zealand sedge make a small, reddish brown mound. In summer it sends up spikes with beige flowers followed by red-brown fruit. The bronze leaves look particularly effective when placed against vivid colors in a border or among tall perennials or shrubs with rich green foliage. Sedges are traditionally regarded as plants that require moist soil, but there are many, such as *Carex flagellifera*, that thrive in drier ground.

OTHER VARIETIES *C. berggrenii* (miniature, with tufts of blue-green leaves); *C. comans* (densely tufted, hairlike yellow-green, gray, or reddish brown leaves); *C. morrowii* 'Fisher' (cream-striped leaves).

PLANT PROFILE
HEIGHT 3½ft (1.1m)
SPREAD 3ft (1m)
SITE Sun or partial shade
SOIL Moist, free-draining
HARDINESS Z7–9 H9–7
FLOWERING Mid- and late summer

C

Carex hachijoensis 'Evergold' Sedge

THIS HIGHLY RATED SEDGE grows wild in Japan on dry, rocky slopes and in woods. Given similar garden conditions and particularly free-draining soil, it makes a beautiful mound of dark green leaves with pale yellow stripes. Its flowers are insignificant compared with the foliage. Plant it in a gravel garden that provides the ideal free-draining soil conditions, while the stony surface sets off the foliage brilliantly. For a taller sedge that requires moist soil, try *Carex elata* 'Aurea' (Bowles' golden sedge), which is about twice the height of 'Evergold' and has arching yellow leaves margined with green.

OTHER VARIETIES *C. petriei* (pale pinkish brown leaves); *C. pendula* (dense clumps of drooping green leaves).

PLANT PROFILE
HEIGHT 12in (30cm)
SPREAD 14in (35cm)
SITE Sun or partial shade
SOIL Free-draining
HARDINESS Z6–9 H9–6
FLOWERING Mid- and late spring

Catananche caerulea Cupid's dart

C

THIS CLUMP-FORMING PLANT has pretty, circular, open flowers that are usually lilac-blue, but can be darker or even white. It is a bright, breezy, cottage garden plant, ideal when a free-flowing display is required. It combines well with 'Bicolor', which is white with a purple eye. Grow Cupid's dart on free-draining soil in a bright, sunny position—when grown on heavier, wetter ground it soon deteriorates and dies. Cupid's dart also makes a good cut flower, brightening up any flower arrangement. Divide clumps every two years, and replant only the younger, fresher, more vigorous growth which will flower more freely.

OTHER VARIETY   *C. caespitosa* (dwarf, yellow flowers in spring).

PLANT PROFILE

HEIGHT	To 3ft (1m)
SPREAD	12in (30cm)
SITE	Full sun
SOIL	Free-draining
HARDINESS	Z5–9 H9–1
FLOWERING	Midsummer to autumn

C

Centaurea macrocephala Knapweed

THIS TALL-GROWING, BOLD PLANT needs a place at the back of the border. Its flowers, just like those of a thistle, are a rich, golden yellow, 2in (5cm) wide, opening on top of strong, stiff stems. The large leaves are rather coarse, but they add to the impact of the flowers. If space allows, there are other knapweeds (many are shorter) with purple, pink, blue, or white flowers. They all need free-draining soil and, while many are drought-tolerant, *Centaurea macrocephala* requires regular watering through the growing season or it will flop.

OTHER VARIETIES (all medium) *C. cineraria* (purple flowers, gray-white leaves); *C. dealbata* (white-centered pink flowers); *C. hypoleuca* 'John Coutts' (deep rose pink flowers).

PLANT PROFILE

HEIGHT To 5ft (1.5m)

SPREAD 24in (60cm)

SITE Sun or partial shade

SOIL Moist but free-draining

HARDINESS Z3–7 H7–1

FLOWERING Midsummer

INVISIBLE SUPPORT

To support a floppy-stemmed plant, use a ring of canes encircled with garden twine. Once the plant fills out, the support will be invisible.

Centaurea montana 'Alba' Mountain knapweed

C

THE VALUE OF THIS KNAPWEED is that it starts flowering in early summer, before the others, and has delicate, open, spiderlike white blooms. It is slightly floppy and sprawling, however, and needs some support to keep it upright. To prevent the appearance of mildew, cut down plants the moment they have finished flowering, which eliminates the problem and promotes new growth. Other colors are available, including 'Carnea' (bright pink), 'Parham' (lavender-blue), and 'Violetta' (dark violet). Free-draining soil that stays moist in summer is essential for mountain knapweeds to flourish.

OTHER VARIETIES (all shorter)   *C. bella* (feathery leaves, pink to purple flowers); *C. pulcherrima* (silvery yellow bracts and pink flowers).

PLANT PROFILE

HEIGHT 18in (45cm)

SPREAD 24in (60cm)

SITE Full sun

SOIL Moist but free-draining

HARDINESS Z4–8

FLOWERING Late spring to midsummer

C

Centranthus ruber Red valerian

A MUST FOR COTTAGE GARDENS, this perennial produces a vigorous clump of crimson flowers on tall thin stems that stand well clear of the foliage. Given modest conditions—it prefers average soil with good drainage—it will produce a superb, free-flowering show throughout the summer. It also self-seeds freely, often in wonderful ways, popping out of stone walls, paving, gravel, and beds. It is a useful plant for making a lively, tasteful link between the formal and wilder, more natural parts of the garden. If you want to prevent it from self-seeding, cut back the flowers as soon as they fade. Pruning also promotes a second flush of blooms.

PLANT PROFILE

HEIGHT To 3ft (1m)

SPREAD To 3ft (1m)

SITE Full sun

SOIL Average, free-draining

HARDINESS Z5–8 H8–5

FLOWERING Spring to late summer

Cephalaria gigantea Giant scabious

C

FOR A LIVELY, IMPRESSIVE DISPLAY, find room in the garden for a giant scabious. It produces a mass of long, thin, stiff-branched stems topped by small pincushion flowers held high above the foliage. Find a gap at the back of a border or cottage garden where it can be seen clearly. It is best grown in rich, moist but well-drained soil, and the plant looks great contrasted with tomato red crocosmias. It can also be used in front of a statue or urn on a plinth, where the ornament will appear to rise up out of a tangle of stems and soft yellow flowers. New plants can be created for additional impact by dividing clumps in the spring or autumn.

OTHER VARIETY *C. alpina* (lower-growing, pale yellow flowers).

PLANT PROFILE

HEIGHT 8ft (2.5m)

SPREAD 24in (60cm)

SITE Sun or partial shade

SOIL Moist but free-draining, fertile

HARDINESS Z3–7 H7–1

FLOWERING Summer

C

Ceratostigma plumbaginoides Leadwort

THE BRIGHT, RICH–COLORED FLOWERS of this plant are a real bonus in a late-season garden, when the leaves also redden up to provide additional interest. This small plant's slim stems creep and crawl, nudging through adjoining plants. It is best appreciated when given a place right at the front of the border, in a rock garden, or on a stone wall, where it will form a mat of growth. When grown in the border, it needs light, free-draining soil and a position sheltered from the effects of cold, wet winters. Young plants need extra protection in their first winter. They can either be potted and brought into a conservatory or greenhouse, or left in the ground and covered with a thick blanket of mulch.

PLANT PROFILE

HEIGHT To 18in (45cm)

SPREAD 12in (30cm) or more

SITE Full sun

SOIL Free-draining

HARDINESS Z5–9 H9–4

FLOWERING Autumn

Chaerophyllum hirsutum 'Roseum' Hairy chervil

C

LOOKING LIKE A PINK VERSION of *Anthriscus sylvestris* (cow parsley), *Chaerophyllum hirsutum* 'Roseum' has similar fernlike leaves and lovely sprays of flowers. It is traditionally grown in wild or cottage gardens, on the freer, outer edge of a formal garden, or backing an artificial pond. The white version is *C. hirsutum*, and both need to be grown in moist soil. If they self-seed, carefully dig up the seedlings in spring and transplant them where needed in the garden. Keep a lookout for slugs and snails, however, because these can devour the new shoots. This plant is sometimes called chervil, but don't confuse it with the herb (*Anthriscus cerefolium*).

PLANT PROFILE
HEIGHT 24in (60cm)
SPREAD 12in (30cm)
SITE Sun or partial shade
SOIL Moist
HARDINESS Z6–9
FLOWERING Late spring to midsummer

C

Chamaemelum nobile 'Flore Pleno' Chamomile

TRADITIONALLY GROWN IN HERB GARDENS or as an edging plant at the front of a border, chamomile spreads well without becoming invasive. 'Flore Pleno' has double white, yellow-eyed flowers, while *Chamaemelum nobile* produces single ones. The leaves of both emit a wonderful scent when crushed and are ideal for a lawn, where plants should be set 5–6in (12–15cm) apart, or a chamomile seat. Water both freely until established, and keep trimming to encourage dense growth. Free-draining sandy soil is ideal, although chamomile will tolerate most sites. The leaves can also be used to make tea, hair rinses, and potpourri. Contact with the leaves can irritate the skin, however, and excessive ingestion can lead to vomiting.

OTHER VARIETY *C. nobile* 'Treneague' (strongly scented foliage).

PLANT PROFILE	
HEIGHT 6in (15cm)	
SPREAD 18in (45cm)	
SITE Sun	
SOIL Free-draining	
HARDINESS Z6–9	
FLOWERING Summer	

Chasmanthium latifolium Sea oats

C

THE COMMON NAME IS A BIT MISLEADING because sea oats is not specifically for coastal gardens. The foliage of this clump-forming North American grass resembles that of a bamboo, and the plant will perform best when planted in moist, rich soil. The flower spikelets appear on slender stems right at the end of the summer or, more commonly, in the autumn, and are initially green but then turn bronze and finally beige. They are worth leaving unpruned throughout winter in the hope that they will be rimed by frost. This also allows the plant to self-seed. If you want to cut the spikelets back at the end of autumn, you can then use them indoors as part of a dried-flower arrangement.

PLANT PROFILE		
HEIGHT 3ft (1m)		
SPREAD 24in (60cm)		
SITE Sun or partial shade		
SOIL Moist, fertile		
HARDINESS Z5–9 H9–5		
FLOWERING Late summer and early autumn		

C

Chelidonium majus 'Flore Pleno' Greater celandine

THIS BRIGHT FLOWER can be grown at the edge of a woodland or on any spare patch of ground in the garden. It is remarkably unfussy and grows just about anywhere, but moist, rich soil in dappled light is ideal. It is said to start flowering when the swallows arrive and stop when they leave, and it certainly does bloom over a long period. It is short-lived but since it self-seeds freely, new plants keep appearing. 'Flore Pleno' has double yellow flowers; *Chelidonium majus* produces single ones.

PLANT PROFILE

HEIGHT 24in (60cm)

SPREAD 8in (20cm)

SITE Sun or light shade

SOIL Moist, fertile

HARDINESS Z5–8 H8–5

FLOWERING Summer

Chelone obliqua Turtlehead

WITH SHOWY, DARK PINK OR PURPLE FLOWERS, said to resemble turtles' heads, this is a good choice for an autumn garden, since the robust blooms can reliably withstand the worsening end-of-season weather. Their warm, rich color makes them a big hit. The packed stems are stiff and erect, and rise up out of a thick mass of lower leaves. Turtlehead prefers rich, moist soil and will even grow in a bog garden, making it a real bonus for anyone with heavy clay soil. If there is any danger that the soil will become too dry, add a thick mulch of compost after the ground has been well watered.

OTHER VARIETY *C. glabra* (pink-tinged white flowers).

PLANT PROFILE

HEIGHT To 24in (60cm)

SPREAD 12in (30cm)

SITE Partial shade or sun

SOIL Moist, fertile

HARDINESS Z3–9 H9–3

FLOWERING Late summer to midautumn

C *Chionochloa conspicua* Plumed tussock grass

THIS PLANT FORMS A TALL TUSSOCK OF STRAPPY, upstanding leaves
with an attractive, reddish brown tinge, although the high point is
in the summer, when the arching flower stems shoot up 6ft (2m).
The flowers resemble those of an open, airy *Cortaderia* (pampas
grass), and the stems make a good cut flower display. A warm,
sheltered site is important in colder regions. Provide free-draining
soil and sand around the neck of the plant to keep it relatively dry
over the winter, and cover plants with a thick layer of mulch in cold
areas as an added safeguard.

PLANT PROFILE
HEIGHT To 6ft (2m)
SPREAD 3ft (1m)
SITE Sun
SOIL Free-draining
HARDINESS Z7–10 H10–7
FLOWERING Mid- and late summer

Pinch out the smaller buds that appear around the larger, central, principal buds. This will increase the size of the flowers that remain.

Chrysanthemum 'Clara Curtis'

C

PLANT PROFILE

A PROFUSE MASS OF DAISYLIKE, SCENTED FLOWERS with green eyes that gradually turn yellow makes this plant special. It is well worth its place in any border for its early autumn display, just when most plants are well past their best. Unlike many chrysanthemums, 'Clara Curtis' needs no pampering in the greenhouse in Zone 5 or above, although it is advisable to mulch over and around the plant with compost to provide extra winter protection. These chrysanthemums are easily propagated by cuttings taken in the spring.

HEIGHT 30in (75cm)	
SPREAD 24in (60cm)	
SITE Full sun	
SOIL Fertile, free-draining	
HARDINESS Z5–9 H9–1	
FLOWERING Late summer to midautumn	

OTHER VARIETIES *C.* 'Mary Stoker' (rose-tinted, apricot-yellow flowers); *C.* 'Nancy Perry'(semidouble, dark pink flowers).

C | *Chrysogonum virginianum* Goldenstar

EQUALLY GOOD IN THE BORDER or as a groundcover plant at the wilder edge of a more formal garden, *Chrysogonum virginianum* has hairy, fresh green leaves and produces yellow, star-shaped flowers throughout the summer. It is not an aggressively invasive plant and can be controlled easily by slicing off the roots with a spade and digging out unwanted growth. It likes rich, moist but free-draining soil and combines well with *Vinca minor* 'Argenteovariegata' (lesser periwinkle), which has blue flowers and creamy variegated foliage. The periwinkle is also a vigorous plant, so when combining these two, periodically cut back the *V. minor* to allow the yellow flowers of *C. virginianum* to show through.

PLANT PROFILE

HEIGHT 10in (25cm)

SPREAD 24in (60cm)

SITE Sun or partial shade

SOIL Fertile, moist but free-draining

HARDINESS Z5–9 H9–2

FLOWERING Early spring to late summer

Cicerbita alpina Sow thistle

C

IMPRESSIVE TALL FLOWER SPIKES carry masses of blue, dandelion-like flowers well above head-height, and make a colorful boundary to a wild garden. The sow thistle can also be grown at the back of a large border, although some people consider its appearance too coarse—especially the long leaves, which can reach 10in (25cm) in length. It likes moist, rich, neutral to acidic soil, and soon self-seeds to create a large display. In windy, exposed sites, the sow thistle may need staking to keep the spikes upright.

OTHER VARIETY *C. plumieri* (smaller-growing, clump-forming blue flowers).

PLANT PROFILE

HEIGHT To 8ft (2.5m)

SPREAD 24in (60cm)

SITE Sun or partial shade

SOIL Moist, fertile

HARDINESS Z5–9 H9–5

FLOWERING Midsummer to early autumn

C

Cichorium intybus Chicory

GROWN WIDELY IN THE MEDITERRANEAN, chicory is suitable for wild or herb gardens (the leaves can be used to make a mild laxative), or even kitchen gardens (the Romans grew it as a vegetable). It prefers full sun but will grow in some shade, and needs fertile, free-draining soil. The blue summer blooms, which can also be pink or white, look a little like dandelion flowers. Add the tender new leaves to salads, or boil them for a few minutes to reduce their bitter taste. The roots of a two-year-old plant can be sliced, roasted, and used with, or instead of, coffee. Those with sensitive skin may find that the plant causes slight irritation.

OTHER VARIETY *C. spinosum* (dwarf with thistlelike blue flowers).

PLANT PROFILE
HEIGHT 4ft (1.2m)
SPREAD 24in (60cm)
SITE Full sun
SOIL Fertile, free-draining
HARDINESS Z4–8 H8–1
FLOWERING Summer

Cimicifuga simplex 'Brunette' Autumn snakeroot

THIS IS A STRIKING BEAUTY with spires of purple-flushed flowers above dark bronze foliage. Look closely and you will see that the flowers have no petals, only stamens, but the effect is just the same. 'White Pearl' is a good close companion because of the contrast between its pure white flowers and the dark foliage of 'Brunette'. It prefers partial shade because the roots grow close to the surface and quickly dry out in hot sun. If grown in a sunnier site, water regularly and cover the soil with a thick mulch. The stems may need staking in windy gardens. Cimicifuga plants may also be sold as *Actaea*.

OTHER VARIETIES *C. japonica* (dark green leaves, pure white flowers); *C. racemosa* (dark green leaves, white flowers in midsummer).

PLANT PROFILE

HEIGHT 3–4ft (1–1.2m)

SPREAD 24in (60cm)

SITE Partial shade

SOIL Moist

HARDINESS Z3–8 H12–1

FLOWERING Early and midautumn

C *Cirsium rivulare* 'Atropurpureum' **Brook thistle**

THIS EASILY GROWN, COLORFUL THISTLE is just about the right size for the majority of garden borders or wild gardens. The ground-level, dark green leaves are 18in (45cm) long, and are more hairy than prickly. The bare, vertical stems that shoot high above the leaves are topped by richly colored flowers, and the plant quickly forms clumps, making an impressive show. Beware of experimenting with other kinds of cirsium because many are very invasive, although the rose pink to lilac *Cirsium japonicum* is one that can be grown in gardens. Both do well in moist but free-draining soil.

PLANT PROFILE

HEIGHT 4ft (1.2m)

SPREAD 24in (60cm)

SITE Full sun

SOIL Moist but free-draining

HARDINESS Z4–8 H8–1

FLOWERING Early and midsummer

Commelina coelestis Day flower

THE COMMON NAME OF THE DAY FLOWER comes from the fact that each bloom lasts only a day, but they form in such rapid succession that there is always a bright blue show. The plant's great virtue is the colorful flowers, which appear late in the season when other plants are fading. The day flower does tend to flop, though, and is typically used as groundcover. Plant it in a warm, sheltered site with free-draining soil, and in colder climates, cover it with a thick, dry winter mulch or pot it and keep it in the greenhouse over the winter. Alternatively, use it as an annual filler for the border.

OTHER VARIETIES *C. tuberosa* (green flowers streaked with dark blue-purple); *C. tuberosa* 'Alba' (white flowers).

PLANT PROFILE

HEIGHT To 3ft (1m)

SPREAD 18in (45cm)

SITE Sun or partial shade

SOIL Free-draining

HARDINESS Z6–10 H12–9

FLOWERING Late summer to midautumn

RHIZOME CUTTINGS

Rhizomes can be divided at any time of year, but after flowering is best. Cut them into about 3in (8cm) sections, each with roots and some dormant buds. Cover the sections with soil mix in a tray and plant out in the autumn once the roots are established and a new shoot is visible.

C | *Convallaria majalis* Lily-of-the-valley

THIS IS A TOP CHOICE for growing in the shade under trees where there is rich, moist soil. The erect pairs of leaves appear in the spring, followed by nodding, white, sweetly scented flowers. Don't hide it too far away in the shade because its beautiful small flowers need to be seen, and it's more vigorous when grown in dappled light. It spreads well but is never invasive, and excess growth can be dug out easily. When picking for cut flower displays, stand the stems in warm water for one to two hours.

OTHER VARIETIES *C. majalis* 'Albostriata' (leaves striped creamy white); *C. majalis* 'Hardwick Hall' (leaves with narrow, pale green margins); *C. majalis* var. *rosea* (pale pink flowers).

PLANT PROFILE	
HEIGHT 9in (23cm)	
SPREAD 12in (30cm)	
SITE Full or partial shade	
SOIL Moist, fertile	
HARDINESS Z2–7 H7–1	
FLOWERING Late spring	

Coreopsis verticillata 'Moonbeam' Tickseed

C

THERE IS AN ATTRACTIVE CONTRAST between the delicate, feathery foliage of this plant and its bright, lemon yellow flowers. It stands up well at the front of a cottage garden or formal border, and provides opportunities for striking color contrasts with reds and blues behind. Adjacent plants should flower in late summer to fill the gap left when the tickseed's blooms come to an end. It prefers free-draining soil but will tolerate heavier ground. 'Zagreb' has golden yellow flowers, and 'Grandiflora' bears dark yellow blooms.

OTHER VARIETIES *C. grandiflora* (taller-growing, yellow flowers); *C. grandiflora* 'Early Sunrise' (semidouble, deep yellow flowers); *C. grandiflora* 'Mayfield Giant' (large, orange-yellow flowers).

PLANT PROFILE	
HEIGHT 20in (50cm)	
SPREAD 18in (45cm)	
SITE Full sun or partial shade	
SOIL Fertile, free-draining	
HARDINESS Z3–9 H9–1	
FLOWERING Early summer	

C

Cortaderia selloana 'Pumila' Pampas grass

THIS STRIKING, STATELY, UPBEAT GRASS has silky plumes that make a real garden focal point. Being so large, it can be used only in sizable borders, and is more often seen growing in a lawn (but beware of its sharp-edged leaves), or by a pond, where it will reflect on the water. It likes free-draining but moist soil, and in colder regions the crowns of young plants needs to be protected in their first winter with a thick mulch. Plumes can be left on all winter; prune them early in the spring before new growth emerges.

OTHER VARIETIES *C. richardii* (taller-growing, earlier-flowering); *C. selloana* 'Aureolineata' (yellow-margined leaves); *C. selloana* 'Rendatleri' (purple-pink heads); *C. selloana* 'Sunningdale Silver' (silver-white plumes).

PLANT PROFILE
HEIGHT 5ft (1.5m)
SPREAD 4ft (1.2m)
SITE Full sun
SOIL Moist but free-draining
HARDINESS Z7–11 H12–1
FLOWERING Late summer

Cortusa matthioli Alpine bells

C

SOMETIMES KNOWN AS ALPINE BELLS, this plant is a low-growing, colorful perennial that is suitable for a shady rock garden or under trees where the soil is moist and rich. Do not try growing *Cortusa matthioli* in a sunny border—it will not survive. The tiny magenta or purple-violet flowers dangle from slim stems and are held above crinkled, hairy leaves, similar to those of a primrose. Divide plants in the spring to increase your stock, and keep a lookout for possible slug and snail attacks.

OTHER VARIETIES *C. matthioli* 'Alba' (white flowers); *C. matthioli* subsp. *pekinensis* (magenta flowers).

PLANT PROFILE	
HEIGHT 8–12in (20–30cm)	
SPREAD 6in (15cm)	
SITE Partial shade	
SOIL Moist, fertile	
HARDINESS Z5–8 H8–5	
FLOWERING Late spring and early summer	

C

Corydalis flexuosa Fumitory

TO PROVIDE A COLORFUL HIGHLIGHT in late spring, the brilliant electric blue flowers of *Corydalis flexuosa* are perfect. It requires a shady spot, whether the sunless side of a stone wall or a shrub, or at the cool, moist end of a border, and is invaluable in cottage gardens because of its mix of leafy growth and small, perky flowers. It mixes well with the bright yellow *C. lutea*, which will also grow in full sun, and both need moist but free-draining soil. Other choices include 'Père David' (mid-blue) and 'China Blue' (pale blue).

OTHER VARIETIES *C. cava* (purple or white flowers); *C. malkensis* (creamy white flowers); *C. ochroleuca* (creamy white flowers with a yellow throat); *C. solida* (mauve-pink to red-purple flowers).

PLANT PROFILE

HEIGHT To 12in (30cm)

SPREAD 8in (20cm)

SITE Partial shade

SOIL Moist but free-draining

HARDINESS Z6–8 H8–6

FLOWERING Late spring to summer

Cosmos atrosanguineus Chocolate cosmos

C

CHOCOLATE-SCENTED FLOWERS make this a novel plant for the garden. It is not a strong scent that wafts around—rather, you have to put your nose into its petals on a hot, sunny day—but it is fun to grow, and the dark maroon flowers are also an unusual color. Grow it among whites, yellows, and pastels to create a contrast. On cold wet clay it will probably die by midwinter. Ideally, plant it in a sunny, sheltered position in moist but well-drained soil, or pot it in the autumn and keep it safe in a greenhouse until spring. Water the pots occasionally throughout the winter so that the soil does not dry out. If left outside all year, add a thick mulch of compost in winter to help the plant to survive.

PLANT PROFILE

HEIGHT 30in (75cm)

SPREAD 18in (45cm)

SITE Full sun

SOIL Moist but free-draining

HARDINESS Z8–11 H12–8

FLOWERING Midsummer to autumn

C

Crambe cordifolia Colewort

THIS MAGNIFICENT PLANT throws out strong, angled, open stems that hold sprays of small, sweetly scented white flowers high above the leaves. Make sure you provide it with plenty of space in the border, where it will create an eye-catching, billowing aerial show of starry blooms. After the display, in the second half of summer, the dark green shiny leaves, which can reach 14in (35cm) wide, become the dominant feature. Free-draining, average soil is the key requirement to success, which is why you often see it thriving in coastal gardens, but it will need some protection in exposed, windy sites.

OTHER VARIETY   *C. maritima* (blue-green leaves and profuse white flowers).

PLANT PROFILE
HEIGHT 8ft (2.5m)
SPREAD 5ft (1.5m)
SITE Full sun or partial shade
SOIL Average, free-draining
HARDINESS Z6–9 H9–6
FLOWERING Late spring and midsummer

Crepis incana Pink dandelion

ORIGINATING IN GREECE, where it grows in rocky, mountainous sites, the pink dandelion ought to be far more popular. The flowers are a rich pink, and the rosettes of hairy leaves are gray-green with jagged edges. The flowers are at their best during the second half of the summer, and add a novel touch to rock or gravel gardens, where the plants will self-seed when the blooms are left unpruned. Bright sun and excellent drainage are essential because if the roots sit in damp soil, they will quickly rot.

OTHER VARIETY *C. aurea* (golden-orange flowers).

PLANT PROFILE	
HEIGHT To 12in (30cm)	
SPREAD To 12in (30cm)	
SITE Full sun	
SOIL Free-draining	
HARDINESS Z5–7 H7–4	
FLOWERING Late summer	

C | *Crocosmia* 'Lucifer' Montbretia

THIS ELECTRIFYINGLY BRIGHT, brief-flowering plant with tomato red flowers has great shock value. The small flowers are borne toward the tips of arching stems and hover in the air, well clear of the ground. The swordlike leaves are bright, fresh green. Place it close to evergreen shrubs that are not in flower to give them a lift, or use it to arch out over ponds, but plant in free-draining soil away from the moist ground by the water's edge. Divide clumps in spring.

OTHER VARIETIES *C.* x *crocosmiiflora* 'Emily McKenzie' (downward-facing, bright orange flowers with maroon markings); *C.* x *crocosmiiflora* 'Jackanapes' (bicolored orange-red and yellow flowers); *C.* x *crocosmiiflora* 'Lady Hamilton' (golden yellow flowers).

PLANT PROFILE	
HEIGHT 3½ft (1.1m)	
SPREAD 8cm (3in)	
SITE Full sun or dappled shade	
SOIL Fertile, free-draining	
HARDINESS Z6–9 H9–2	
FLOWERING Mid- to late summer	

Cynara cardunculus Cardoon

C

THIS IS THE ULTIMATE THISTLE. A superb perennial, it spires straight up, firing out huge, horizontal, silver-gray leaves, nearly 24in (60cm) long and 14in (35cm) wide. The rich purple flowers are held on top of strong, straight stems. Place it at the back of a wide border, but make sure the plants in front don't obscure it. Alternatively, grow it as a feature plant in a wild part of the garden. Leave the stems over winter as an architectural, skeletal shape, but cut them down before the new growth starts in spring. It grows well in free-draining soil, which you should enrich each spring by forking in well-rotted manure around the root area, but not close to the crown.

OTHER VARIETY *C. scolymus* (edible flower buds, purple flowers).

PLANT PROFILE

HEIGHT 5ft (1.5m)

SPREAD 4ft (1.2m)

SITE Full sun

SOIL Free-draining

HARDINESS Z7–9 H9–7

FLOWERING Early summer to early autumn

C

Cynoglossum nervosum Hound's tongue

THIS IS JUST ABOUT THE ONLY perennial hound's tongue grown in gardens. Similar to the forget-me-not (*Myosotis*), it features sprays of small blue flowers above bristly stems and hairy leaves. It is perfectly happy on average, even poor ground (avoid heavy clay and very fertile conditions), but will do best in moist but free-draining soil. The blue flowers mix well with the white flowers of snow-in-summer (*Cerastium tomentosum*), but make sure it does not become swamped by this vigorous, spreading plant.

OTHER VARIETY   *C. amabile* (taller-growing, blue flowers, occasionally pink or white).

PLANT PROFILE
HEIGHT 24in (60cm)
SPREAD 24in (60cm)
SITE Sun or partial shade
SOIL Average, moist but free-draining
HARDINESS Z5–8
FLOWERING Midspring to midsummer

Dactylis glomerata 'Variegata' Orchard grass

D

IN THE WILD THIS GRASS is used for grazing, and it can often be seen growing by the sides of roads. In the garden, however, it needs some pampering to keep it looking neat. Groom out the dead leaves in the spring and autumn (use your splayed, open fingers to comb them out), and the brightly variegated foliage will give you a good show in return. *Dactylis glomerata* 'Variegata' forms a dense tuft, and the pale green flower spikes appear throughout the summer. The stems can be left standing over the winter months and cut back the following spring before the new shoots emerge.

PLANT PROFILE

HEIGHT To 18in (45cm)

SPREAD 10in (25cm)

SITE Sun or partial shade

SOIL Fertile, free-draining

HARDINESS Z5–9 H9–5

FLOWERING Summer

Store tubers over winter in a cool, frost-free place. When the leaves are blackened by frost, cut the stems down, ease the tubers out of the ground, and remove excess soil. Place the tubers upside down for about 3 weeks in a box. Once dry, dust with fungicide and place the stems, right side up, in bark chips. Keep them dry until ready to plant out again in late spring.

D

Dahlia 'Bishop of Llandaff'

SOME OF THE MOST EXCITING FLOWER COLORS are provided by dahlias. They come in rich reds and purples, yellows and oranges, as well as paler shades, with flowers in all shapes and sizes. 'Bishop of Llandaff' has bright red flowers, set against dark, almost black, shiny leaves. It is perfect for a fiery summer border or a gravel garden, where its beautiful foliage contrasts well with the light stones. Plant out the tubers in free-draining soil in spring when there is no further danger of frost.

OTHER VARIETIES *D.* 'Chimborazo' (dark maroon flowers with yellow centers); *D.* 'Davenport Sunlight' (vivid yellow flowers); *D.* 'Hamari Bride' (pure white flowers); *D.* 'Wootton Cupid' (sugar pink flowers).

PLANT PROFILE

HEIGHT 3½ft (1.1m)

SPREAD 18in (45cm)

SITE Full sun

SOIL Fertile, free-draining

HARDINESS Z9–11 H12–1

FLOWERING Midsummer to late autumn

Darmera peltata Umbrella plant

D

SOMETIMES CALLED THE UMBRELLA PLANT, this slowly spreading perennial forms a striking umbrella-like clump of dark green leaves up to 18in (45cm) wide, which turn a wonderful ruby red in the autumn. The leaves are preceded in spring by the flowers, which make flat heads of pale pink. It is suitable for planting in a pond or by the edge of a stream, where its creeping roots will help to bind the muddy soil and prevent it from being eroded by the moving water. Established clumps can be divided in the spring, but don't be tempted to replant them near a small pond because they will soon outgrow the space and swamp the water feature.

PLANT PROFILE

HEIGHT To 6ft (2m)

SPREAD 3ft (1m)

SITE Sun or partial shade

SOIL Wet

HARDINESS Z5–9 H9–5

FLOWERING Late spring

D | *Delphinium* 'Black Knight' Delphinium

DELPHINIUMS ARE A FANTASTIC SIGHT in the garden, where they make clumps of tall, upright spires clothed in cup-shaped flowers. 'Black Knight' is a striking, dark purple example, perfect for the back of a cottage garden–style border, where it can be mixed with contrasting pink, white, and red flowers. Stake plants in exposed, windy sites, and protect them from slugs, especially in spring as the young growth emerges. There are dozens of other blues to choose from, including the mid-blue 'Blue Nile' and pale blue 'Skyline'.

OTHER VARIETIES *D.* 'Blue Dawn' (pale blue flowers); *D.* Belladonna Group 'Casa Blanca' (white flowers); *D.* 'Emily Hawkins' (violet flowers); *D.* 'Rosemary Brock' (deep pink flowers); *D.* 'Tiddles' (mauve flowers).

PLANT PROFILE
HEIGHT 4–5ft (1.2–1.5m)
SPREAD 24in (60cm)
SITE Full sun
SOIL Fertile, free-draining
HARDINESS Z3–7
FLOWERING Early to midsummer

Deschampsia cespitosa 'Goldschleier' Tufted hair grass

D

THIS EXCELLENT GRASS has long, thin, strappy green leaves, and in summer produces dozens of erect stems with tiny, silver-tinged purple flowers that turn silvery and then beige. Leave the stems through winter to add extra shape to the garden, but cut them off the following spring before the new growth emerges. The silvery flowers stand out best against a dark background, such as a thick beech hedge. Tufted hair grass is happy in most soils, including clay that has had lots of compost added to it to improve the drainage.

OTHER VARIETIES *D. cespitosa* (taller-growing); *D. cespitosa* 'Goldtau' (compact, with silvery reddish brown flowers); *D. flexuosa* 'Tatra Gold' (yellow-green leaves, bronze-tinted flowers).

PLANT PROFILE

HEIGHT To 4ft (1.2m)

SPREAD To 4ft (1.2m)

SITE Sun or partial shade

SOIL Free-draining

HARDINESS Z4–9

FLOWERING Early to late summer

D

Dianthus 'Doris' Carnation

AVAILABLE IN A WIDE COLOR RANGE, from white ('Hatyor White') to flashy red and yellow ('Bookham Fancy'), carnations, or pinks, are quintessential cottage garden plants. Many emit a sweet scent of cloves—the old-fashioned types, such as the white 'Mrs Sinkins', have the best scent, although many modern hybrids, such as 'Doris', are also perfumed. All need free-draining soil; without it, grow them in a raised bed, rock garden, or tub. Deadheading encourages a long succession of flowers throughout the summer.

OTHER VARIETIES *D.* 'Dad's Favorite' (semidouble, white flowers); *D.* 'Inchmery' (double, lavender-pink flowers); *D.* 'Monica Wyatt' (double, pale lavender-pink flowers with magenta centers.).

PLANT PROFILE

HEIGHT 10–18in (25–45cm)

SPREAD 16in (40cm)

SITE Full sun

SOIL Free-draining

HARDINESS Z5–9 H8–1

FLOWERING Summer

Diascia 'Blackthorn Apricot' Twinspur

D

MAKING A CLUMP OF VERTICAL SPIKES of pastel-colored flowers, this is one of the best perennials for nonstop summer flowering and is great for the front of a border. Cut it back in midsummer to prevent it from becoming straggly and to encourage even more blooms. It needs a sheltered, free-draining site, or dig up a clump in autumn for potting and overwintering in the greenhouse. Alternatively, take cuttings in early summer to produce new plants. While free-draining soil is important, diascias need a regular water supply throughout the summer.

OTHER VARIETIES *D. integerrima* (purplish pink flowers); *D. barberae* 'Ruby Field' (rich salmon pink flowers).

PLANT PROFILE
HEIGHT 10in (25cm)
SPREAD To 20in (50cm)
SITE Full sun
SOIL Free-draining
HARDINESS Z8–9 H9–8
FLOWERING Summer to autumn

D

Dicentra 'Langtrees' Bleeding heart

THIS DAPPLED-SHADE- AND MOISTURE-LOVING PLANT is particularly suitable for cottage gardens and formal borders. Some varieties of dicentra shoot everywhere, but 'Langtrees' is a short, compact, noninvasive spreader with pink-tinged flowers. It can be grown close to *Dicentra spectabilis,* where its tall arching stems of pink, dangling flowers will create a light canopy above 'Langtrees'. Both dicentras make successful groundcover in gardens where the soil never dries out.

OTHER VARIETIES *D.* 'Adrian Bloom' (rich red flowers); *D.* 'Bacchanal' (crimson flowers); *D.* 'Bountiful' (purple-pink flowers); *D.* 'Luxuriant' (red flowers); *D.* 'Stuart Boothman' (deep pink flowers).

PLANT PROFILE
HEIGHT 12in (30cm)
SPREAD 18in (45cm)
SITE Partial shade
SOIL Moist
HARDINESS Z3–8 H10–1
FLOWERING Midspring to midsummer

Dictamnus albus var. *purpureus* Burning bush

THIS IS A TRUE CONVERSATION PIECE of a perennial. On warm summer evenings, it releases tiny amounts of volatile oil—to see how its common name came about, simply light a match at the base and watch how intermittent spurts of flame are produced. It looks a little like the flicker of flame produced when you ignite the brandy in a dish of cherries jubilee. Even if the trick does not work, it is still a choice garden plant. Tall and stately, it has leathery leaves smelling of lemons when crushed, and spikes of purple-mauve flowers, followed by seed pods that erupt and catapult seed all around when ripe. Give it rich, fertile, free-draining soil and select the right position the first time, because it dislikes being moved once it's established.

PLANT PROFILE

HEIGHT 16–36in (40–90cm)

SPREAD 24in (60cm)

SITE Full sun or partial shade

SOIL Fertile, free-draining

HARDINESS Z5–8 H8–1

FLOWERING Early summer

D

Dierama pulcherrimum Angel's fishing rod

THIS STAR PLANT HAS ARCHING, graceful flower stems that ascend out of a central, evergreen clump of foliage. The dangling bell-shaped flowers are about 2in (5cm) long and sway in the wind, bringing color and movement to the garden. Plant it toward the front of a border where it can arch over a wide path, or site it by a pond to overhang the water. It needs moist, rich soil and a sheltered position, and young plants may take a few years to flower. When it is well established, you can divide clumps in the spring.

OTHER VARIETIES *D. pulcherrimum* 'Blackbird' (rich purple flowers); *D. pendulum* (purple-pink flowers); *D. dracomontanum* (pink to red flowers).

PLANT PROFILE
HEIGHT 3–5ft (1–1.5m)
SPREAD 24in (60cm)
SITE Full sun
SOIL Moist, fertile
HARDINESS Z8–10 H10–8
FLOWERING Summer

Digitalis x *mertonensis* Foxglove

D

MOST FOXGLOVES ARE BIENNIALS (growing, flowering, and dying in two years), but this is a short-lived perennial, with spires of large, open-mouthed, strawberry pink flowers that are loved by bees. The dark green leaves make a good contrast. It will flourish when grown on the shady side of the garden, or close to a woodland setting. Any seedlings can be carefully forked out of the ground and transplanted to other parts of the garden, or you can collect seed in the autumn and sow it in pots. Keep in a cold frame over the winter.

OTHER VARIETIES *D. davisiana* (pale yellow flowers); *D. ferruginea* (golden brown flowers veined with red-brown); *D. grandiflora* (pale yellow flowers); *D. parviflora* (dark orange-brown flowers).

PLANT PROFILE
HEIGHT To 3ft (1m)
SPREAD 12in (30cm)
SITE Partial shade
SOIL Moist, fertile
HARDINESS Z3–8 H8–1
FLOWERING Late spring and early sumer

D | *Disporopsis pernyi* Fairy bells

THIS REMARKABLY EASY TO-GROW PERENNIAL does best if provided with moist but well-drained soil either in a shady part of the garden or on the shady side of an evergreen shrub. It has decorative mottled stems and produces shiny, dark green leaves that remain evergreen, unless caught in freezing temperatures. The lemon-scented flowers are flared at the tips, and appear in late spring or early summer. You can easily obtain more plants by dividing the bulblike underground growths in the spring, but make sure that each division has at least one good shoot and its own roots.

PLANT PROFILE
HEIGHT 16in (40cm)
SPREAD 12–16in (30–40cm)
SITE Partial shade
SOIL Moist but free-draining
HARDINESS Z7–9 H9–7
FLOWERING Early summer

Dodecatheon meadia f. *album* Shooting stars

THE SWEPT-BACK PETALS of the dodecatheons account for their common name. This eye-catching plant produces a clump of leaves, about 8in (20cm) long, which burst out of the ground with the strong, thin, flowering stems. Grow it in a shady rock garden, or under trees, where its delicate flowers combine well with bluebells, which enjoy the same rich, moist but well-drained soil conditions. Beware of slugs and snails—they can ruin the display.

OTHER VARIETIES *D. clevelandii* (reddish purple flowers);
D. hendersonii (crimson-pink flowers); *D. dentatum* (shorter with white flowers); *D. pulchellum* (deep cerise pink flowers with dark centers).

PLANT PROFILE	
HEIGHT 16in (40cm)	
SPREAD 10in (25cm)	
SITE Partial shade	
SOIL Moist but free-draining, fertile	
HARDINESS Z4–8 H8–1	
FLOWERING Mid- and late spring	

D | *Doronicum orientale* 'Magnificum' Leopard's bane

THESE QUINTESSENTIAL SPRING PLANTS produce large, daisylike, bright yellow blooms, held well clear of the foliage. Leopard's bane is extremely easy to grow in most gardens, especially in the middle of a border or wild area, and likes moist but free-draining soil. It also makes a lively backdrop to a wide assortment of spring bulbs. Plant 'Magnificum' close to neighbors that offer eye-catching flowers in mid- to late summer, because it tends to die down at this time. Other forms of *Doronicum orientale* offer lemon yellow flowers ('Gerhard') and double flowers ('Frühlingspracht').

OTHER VARIETIES *D. columnae* 'Miss Mason' (large, bright yellow flowers); *D. x excelsum* 'Harpur Crewe' (larger-growing).

PLANT PROFILE
HEIGHT 20in (50cm)
SPREAD 3ft (1m)
SITE Partial shade
SOIL Moist but free-draining
HARDINESS Z5–7
FLOWERING Mid- and late spring

Dracunculus vulgaris Dragon arum

THERE ARE THREE GOOD REASONS for growing this perennial. First, the mottled shoots emerge from the ground looking like snakes; second, the astonishing flowers last for a week and immediately catch the eye; and, third, the incredibly disgusting scent is like that of a putrid drain, and is often a big hit with children. The rotten smell is designed to attract pollinating insects in the Mediterranean countries where it grows naturally. It will survive in cooler climates in well-drained soil that becomes quite dry in summer, and when given a protective winter mulch of compost. For plants with similar flowers, but without the smell, try arums.

PLANT PROFILE

HEIGHT To 5ft (1.5m)

SPREAD 24in (60cm)

SITE Full sun

SOIL Fertile, free-draining

HARDINESS Z8–10 H10–8

FLOWERING Spring or summer

Echinacea purpurea Coneflower

NEITHER SUBTLE NOR SHY, this plant has large pink flowers with central, golden orange-brown cones that are loved by bees and butterflies. Standing upright without staking, the coneflower adds color and substance to borders in cottage or gravel gardens in the second half of summer. It thrives in fertile, well-drained soil and sun, and stocks can be increased easily by dividing plants in the spring or autumn. Other useful colors to combine with this one include white, pinkish crimson, and dark orange.

OTHER VARIETIES *E. purpurea* 'Magnus' (extra-large, dark orange flowers); *E. purpurea* 'White Lustre' (creamy white flowers).

PLANT PROFILE

HEIGHT 5ft (1.5m)

SPREAD 18in (45cm)

SITE Full sun

SOIL Fertile, free-draining

HARDINESS Z4–9 H9–2

FLOWERING Midsummer to early autumn

Once the seedheads are dry and have turned brown, cut off the stems and pick off the seeds. Place them in a paper bag to dry and store until you are ready to sow them in a seedbed in the spring.

Echinops bannaticus 'Taplow Blue' Globe thistle

E

SPHERICAL, BRIGHT BLUE FLOWERS, about 2in (5cm) wide, on top of sturdy, thin stems provide an extra dimension to the middle or back of a border. The flowers are held high above jagged, spiny, hairy, gray green leaves, and the plants soon form decent clumps when grown on dry, free-draining soil. Globe thistles are susceptible to mildew and if badly affected may need to be sprayed in late summer with a fungicide. Other choices include 'Blue Globe', with dark blue flowers, and the shorter *Echinops ritro*, with bright blue globes.

OTHER VARIETIES *E. bannaticus* (blue-gray flowers); *E. ritro* 'Veitch's Blue' (smaller-growing, dark blue flowers); *E. sphaerocephalus* (vigorous, gray flowers).

PLANT PROFILE
HEIGHT 5ft (1.5m)
SPREAD 24in (60cm)
SITE Full sun
SOIL Free-draining
HARDINESS Z3–9 H12–1
FLOWERING Mid- and late summer

E

Echium pininana Giant viper's bugloss

ALTHOUGH IT TAKES THREE YEARS TO FLOWER and then immediately dies, it is well worth the wait just to see the Canary Island *Echium pininana* in its full glory. It forms a rosette of dark green, hairy leaves about 3in (7cm) long, out of which shoots an astonishing stem, 5-12ft (1.5-4m) high, covered with bluey mauve flowers. A mild climate without hard frosts is essential for it to survive the winter, and it likes free-draining, reasonably fertile soil. Given these conditions, it will self-seed after flowering. This amazing plant fits into the category of "astonishingly exotic," and probably "extremely odd" to anyone who prefers traditional borders, but it is a must for lovers of striking, architectural plants.

PLANT PROFILE

HEIGHT To 12ft (4m)

SPREAD 3ft (1m)

SITE Full sun

SOIL Fertile, free-draining

HARDINESS Z9–10 H10–9

FLOWERING Mid- and late summer

Elymus magellanicus Wild rye

E

WITH ITS ASTONISHING, INTENSE BLUE LEAVES, this is a grass with real panache. Scattering gravel around the plant highlights its color. It needs excellent drainage—slopes provide an ideal site—and as well as hating cold, wet winter soil, it also dislikes hot, humid nights. The leaves may discolor if attacked by rust, but this is no reason for not growing it. During mild winters, the leaves remain evergreen, adding color to the winter garden, while in cold-climate gardens you can cut off the foliage in the autumn. Spring is the best time to divide clumps.

OTHER VARIETIES *E. canadensis* (taller-growing, blue-green leaves, dense green flower spikes); *E. hispidus* (pale silvery blue leaves).

PLANT PROFILE	
5HEIGHT 6in (15cm)	
SPREAD 12in (30cm)	
SITE Full sun	
SOIL Free-draining	
HARDINESS Z7–8	
FLOWERING Summer	

E

Eomecon chionantha Snow poppy

THE SNOW POPPY is nothing like a traditional poppy, largely because it is a quick-spreading, invasive perennial with kidney shaped leaves up to 4in (10cm) wide. The white, four-petaled flowers have a yellow center, and are individually attractive, although the plant needs hot weather in order to flower freely in the early summer. It makes good groundcover when grown on moist but free-draining soil that never dries out, even in summer—for example, on a shady bank or in a shrub border. The more fertile the soil, the more prolifically it will spread.

PLANT PROFILE
HEIGHT 16in (40cm)
SPREAD Indefinite
SITE Light shade or full sun
SOIL Fertile, moist but free-draining
HARDINESS Z7–9 H9–7
FLOWERING Late spring to midsummer

Epilobium angustifolium var. *album* Willow herb

E

THIS COTTAGE-GARDEN FAVORITE has spires of white flowers blooming above the foliage and makes a lively background to reds and bright blues. It quickly multiplies, creating large clumps, and spreads by seed and underground roots. You can stop willow herb from spreading excessively by cutting off the flowers as soon as they start to fade, thus eliminating the seed. You can also slice the roots with a spade and dig out any unwanted growth. Slugs and snails can attack the stems but, given its prolific nature, they rarely become a real problem. Willow herb likes moist but free-draining soil.

OTHER VARIETIES *E. dodonaei* (pinkish purple flowers); *E. glabellum* (creamy white or pink flowers).

PLANT PROFILE
HEIGHT To 5ft (1.5m)
SPREAD 3ft (1m)
SITE Full sun or partial shade
SOIL Moist but free-draining
HARDINESS Z3–7 H7–1
FLOWERING Midsummer to early autumn

Epimedium pinnatum subsp. *colchicum* Barrenwort

TINY, ALMOST ORCHIDLIKE FLOWERS, sometimes with long spurs, consisting of four flat, oval, bright yellow petals grace this plant. The flowers range up the stems, above the dark, evergreen, heart-shaped leaves that form a large clump at the base. It thrives in rich soil under trees or near evergreen shrubs that provide shelter against cold winds. If grown in more open, sunnier ground, the soil needs to be covered with a thick mulch of compost to lock in moisture. Cut back the leaves in late winter or early spring.

OTHER VARIETIES *E. grandiflorum* (white, yellow, pink, or purple flowers); *E.* x *perralchicum* (larger-growing, bright yellow flowers); *E.* x *youngianum* 'Niveum' (pure white flowers).

PLANT PROFILE

HEIGHT 12–16in (30–40cm)

SPREAD 10in (25cm)

SITE Partial shade

SOIL Moist, fertile, free-draining

HARDINESS Z5–9 H9–4

FLOWERING Spring

Eremurus robustus Foxtail lily

E

SPIRES OF TINY, PALE PINK FLOWERS make an eye-catching sight at the back of a border in a cottage-style or gravel garden. This is a tall eremurus, and it associates well in the garden with the shorter types, such as the yellow *Eremurus stenophyllus* and white *E. himalaicus*. Foxtail lilies are quite fussy and demand fertile, free-draining soil and a warm, sheltered site. Staking is important to ensure that the flower spires stand tall and erect, especially in exposed sites.

PLANT PROFILE
HEIGHT To 10ft (3m)
SPREAD To 4ft (1.2m)
SITE Full sun
SOIL Fertile, free-draining
HARDINESS Z5–8 H8–5
FLOWERING Early and midsummer

OTHER VARIETY *E. x isabellinus* 'Cleopatra' (orange flowers).

Erigeron 'Dunkelste Aller' Fleabane

THESE COLORFUL FLOWERS have a yellow center and petals that are a rich, dark violet (in German, "Dunkelste Aller" means "darkest of all"). Given free-draining soil and some midday shade, it makes a strong show in early summer, but water well in prolonged periods of drought. It associates well with pink and white erigerons in a formal or cottage-style garden. Deadheading promotes extra flowers, and division every three years maintains the plant's vigor.

OTHER VARIETIES *E.* 'Charity' (semidouble, lilac-pink flowers); *E.* 'Prosperity' (almost double, mauve-blue flowers); *E.* 'Quakeress' (pink-flushed white flowers); *E.* 'Wuppertal' (semidouble, dark lilac flowers).

PLANT PROFILE
HEIGHT 24in (60cm)
SPREAD 18in (45cm)
SITE Full sun
SOIL Free-draining
HARDINESS Z5–8 H8–5
FLOWERING Early and midsummer

E

Eriophyllum lanatum Golden yarrow

THIS BRIGHT, FLASHY YELLOW PLANT is suitable for rock and gravel gardens, stone walls, terraces, and as edging at the front of a border. It is well worth growing if you can provide excellent drainage coupled with average-to-poor soil. The leaves are 3in (8cm) long, and stems are abundantly covered with open, daisylike flowers with darker yellow eyes. Being drought-tolerant, it is easy to grow and makes a fun display when planted in cracks in a patio. Take precautions against attacks from slugs and snails, and when growing golden yarrow in rock gardens, leave space for it to spread or it will soon swamp its neighbors.

PLANT PROFILE

HEIGHT 16in (40cm)

SPREAD 16in (40cm)

SITE Full sun

SOIL Average, free-draining

HARDINESS Z5–8 H8–5

FLOWERING Late spring to summer

E | *Erodium chrysanthum* **Heron's bill**

SIMILAR TO A GERANIUM (cranesbill), the flowers of this perennial give way to berries with a long beak, or bill. The summer-long flowers are pale yellow and blend beautifully with the attractive, silver-green leaves. Originally coming from rocky sites in Greece, it hates wet winters and requires gritty soil with excellent drainage. Grow it in a trough or rockery, raised bed, or gap in a terrace or patio paving. It can be potted in the autumn and kept over the winter in the greenhouse to prevent it from rotting in wet soil.

OTHER VARIETIES *E. cheilanthifolium* (pale pink or white flowers with red veins); *E. corsicum* (rose pink flowers with darker veins); *E. glandulosum* (lilac-pink flowers); *E. manescaui* (magenta-purple flowers).

PLANT PROFILE
HEIGHT 6in (15cm)
SPREAD 16in (40cm)
SITE Full sun
SOIL Fertile, free-draining
HARDINESS Z7–8 H8–7
FLOWERING Summer

Eryngium variifolium Sea holly

E

ARCHITECTURAL, QUIRKY, AND FUN, there is a wide range of sea hollies, many with blue or silvery tints, and all with striking flowers. *Eryngium variifolium* forms a mass of sharp-tipped spines and must be kept away from the edge of a border where young children play, but position it where it can still be seen clearly. It is strange and shapely, with white-veined leaves at soil level, and stiff, branched stems. Ideal for coastal gardens with poor soil and sharp drainage, but will need a warm, sheltered site in colder areas.

OTHER VARIETIES *E. bourgatii* (gray-green flowers); *E. bourgatii* 'Oxford Blue' (silvery blue flowers); *E. giganteum* (taller-growing, steel blue flowers); *E. x oliverianum* (bright silver-blue flowers).

PLANT PROFILE

HEIGHT 12–16in (30–40cm)

SPREAD 10in (25cm)

SITE Full sun

SOIL Free-draining

HARDINESS Z5–9 H9–5

FLOWERING Mid- and late summer

E | *Erysimum* 'Bowles Mauve' Wallflower

THRIVING HAPPILY IN THE CRACKS of a stone wall, this plant lives up to its common name of "wallflower." Adding color and a sweet, pervasive scent, it is also a favorite for the front of a border or an island bed planted with spring bedding. The only problem is that it is very short-lived—four years with good luck and a very light, free-draining soil—but replacement cuttings are easy to take. There are many fine alternatives, in a range of colors from white to red, all of which create a lively display.

OTHER VARIETIES *E.* 'Bredon' (rich yellow flowers); *E. cheiri* 'Harpur Crewe' (double, yellow flowers); *E. linifolium* 'Variegatum' (mauve flowers, white-variegated leaves); *E.* 'Moonlight' (sulfur yellow flowers).

PLANT PROFILE
HEIGHT 30in (75cm)
SPREAD 24in (60cm)
SITE Full sun
SOIL Free-draining
HARDINESS Z5–8 H8–5
FLOWERING Late winter to summer

Erythronium 'Pagoda' Dog's-tooth violet

E

A SUPERB SPRING PERENNIAL, 'Pagoda' has a combination of yellow flowers and bright green leaves. A delicate-looking beauty, it needs to be planted in front of, and shaded by, border shrubs in what equates to a woodland site. It likes moisture throughout the year, so don't let it bake over summer. Other good choices include *Erythronium dens-canis*, with white, pink, or lilac flowers, and *E. revolutum*, which has swept-back, pinky white petals with a yellow center.

OTHER VARIETIES *E. californicum* (creamy white flowers with brownish orange markings); *E. dens-canis* 'Pink Perfection' (clear pink flowers); *E. dens-canis* 'Snowflake' (pure white flowers); *E.* 'Kondo' (scented, lemon yellow flowers); *E. tuolumnense* (bright yellow flowers).

PLANT PROFILE	
HEIGHT 6–14in (15–35cm)	
SPREAD 4in (10cm)	
SITE Partial shade	
SOIL Moist, fertile	
HARDINESS Z4–9 H9–1	
FLOWERING Spring	

E

Eupatorium purpureum subsp. *maculatum* 'Atropurpureum' Joe Pye weed

THIS BIG PLANT for a large border or wild garden looks its best in the second half of summer, when it forms massive clumps. Coming from damp sites in eastern North America, it also likes bog gardens and sites near streams and natural ponds. If it is grown in borders, the soil must not bake dry or it will flop. The flowers attract bees and butterflies, and appear in flat clusters just above the foliage on stiff, purplish stems. Use this plant in bold groups with other late-summer big-hitters, such as rudbeckias, which also like damp soil.

OTHER VARIETIES *E. album* 'Braunlaub' (brown-flushed leaves and flowers); *E. cannabinum* (smaller-growing, pink, purple, or white flowers); *E. rugosum* (pure white flowers).

PLANT PROFILE
HEIGHT 7ft (2.2m)
SPREAD 3ft (1m)
SITE Full sun or partial shade
SOIL Damp, fertile
HARDINESS Z3–7 H7–1
FLOWERING Midsummer to early autumn

Euphorbia dulcis 'Chameleon' Spurge

E

MAKE SURE YOU BUY 'Chameleon' rather than the parent, *Euphorbia dulcis*, as the former has marvelous purple foliage right through the summer that flares up even more in the autumn, making it one of the most eye-catching spurges. By cutting it back after flowering, you can promote a second, fresh batch of leaves. Plant it at the front of a border or by a path, in moist, rich soil and some light shade. Wear gloves when handling or pruning because the sap can irritate the skin and eyes, and all parts of the plant are poisonous.

OTHER VARIETIES *E. amygdaloides* var. *robbiae* (leathery, dark green leaves); *E. griffithii* 'Fireglow' (orange-red bracts around flowerheads); *E. palustris* (bright green leaves, yellow bracts).

PLANT PROFILE	
HEIGHT 12in (30cm)	
SPREAD 12in (30cm)	
SITE Dappled shade	
SOIL Moist, fertile	
HARDINESS Z4–9 H9–1	
FLOWERING Early summer	

E

Euphorbia polychroma Spurge

AT ITS PEAK AT THE END OF SPRING, this evergreen spurge with its bright greenish yellow bracts combines well with bright red tulips, and enlivens borders in the lull between the main spring show and early summer flowers. Its compact foliage makes an attractive low mound throughout the year, and in the autumn the foliage can display red and purple hues. This spurge is happy in a range of soils but does best in sun. Other good choices include 'Major', which grows slightly taller, and 'Candy', which has a purple tinge in spring. Wear gloves when handling spurge because the sap irritates the skin.

OTHER VARIETIES *E. dulcis* 'Chameleon' (purple leaves, yellow-green bracts); *E. griffithii* 'Dixter' (coppery dark green leaves, orange bracts).

PLANT PROFILE

HEIGHT 16in (40cm)	
SPREAD 24in (60cm)	
SITE Full sun	
SOIL Moist, free-draining	
HARDINESS Z5–9 H9–5	
FLOWERING Midspring to midsummer	

Ferula communis Giant fennel

F

THIS HIGHLY IMPRESSIVE BORDER PLANT should not be confused with the fennel used for cooking. Its delightful, feathery leaves can reach a huge 18in (45cm) in length, although there is a slow buildup, possibly taking a couple of years, before the tall flower stems, topped by a scattering of yellow flowers, make their appearance. It is such a climactic performance that the plant may then die after scattering new seed around, or take another couple of years to flower again. Grow giant fennel in reasonably fertile, well-drained soil in a sunny, protected site in colder zones, and protect the crown of the plant with mulch over the winter.

OTHER VARIETY *F. communis* subsp. *glauca* (blue flowers).

PLANT PROFILE

HEIGHT To 15ft (5m)

SPREAD 10–18in (25–45cm)

SITE Full sun

SOIL Fertile

HARDINESS Z6–9 H9–6

FLOWERING Early and midsummer

F

Festuca glauca 'Blaufuchs' Blue fescue

THE FLOWERS CANNOT COMPETE with the show of bright silver-blue, evergreen leaves that splay out to resemble the spines of a porcupine. Grow it in imaginative plans, positioned at the front of a border, or alternating with other shapely plants in average to poor, free-draining soil. Mediterranean-type gardens are an ideal setting, alongside pots of unusual cacti. After a few years, the foliage color tends to fade, but dividing and replanting the vigorous outer portions will provide a fresh supply of plants.

OTHER VARIETIES *F. amethystina* (dense gray-green leaves); *F. eskia* (smaller-growing, rich green leaves); *F. valesiaca* 'Silbersee' (compact, pale silvery blue leaves).

PLANT PROFILE

HEIGHT To 12in (30cm)

SPREAD 10in (25cm)

SITE Sun

SOIL Average, free-draining

HARDINESS Z4–8 H8–1

FLOWERING Early and midsummer

Filipendula rubra 'Venusta' Queen of the prairie

THIS TALL, VIGOROUS SPREADER adds an attractive presence to bog gardens, the banks of streams, or wild gardens. The leafy red stems grow some 6ft (2m) high, with feathery flower plumes, similar in appearance to those of an astilbe, appearing just above them. This plant needs plenty of space, but if it spreads too far, slice off the snaking, shallow roots with a spade and dig out the excess growth. *Filipendula palmata* is more suitable for small gardens, reaching only 4ft (1.2m) high and 24in (60cm) wide.

OTHER VARIETIES *F. purpurea* (smaller-growing, carmine red flowers); *F. ulmaria* (smaller-growing, creamy white flowers); *F. vulgaris* 'Multiplex' (double creamy white flowers from bronze buds).

PLANT PROFILE

HEIGHT 6–8ft (2–2.5m)

SPREAD 4ft (1.2m)

SITE Full sun or partial shade

SOIL Moist, free-draining

HARDINESS Z3–9 H9–1

FLOWERING Early and midsummer

F

Foeniculum vulgare 'Purpureum' Bronze fennel

THIS EXTREMELY USEFUL HERB can be grown in herb gardens or in borders, either right at the front, where it provides a see-through, feathery curtain of leaves, or, because of its height, at the back, where it can be seen clearly. It is an easy plant to grow and, although the soil should be free-draining, it tolerates heavier clay. The yellow summer flowers are on the insipid side, and can be snipped off to prevent self-seeding. While it can be grown as an ornamental plant, the leaves are also suitable for cooking. Pick and place them under a roast chicken, where they lose their aniseed flavor and become quite nutty, enriching the juices. *Foeniculum vulgare* var. *dulce* (Florence fennel) is grown for its crisp, underground bulb, which is used in stews and salads.

PLANT PROFILE

HEIGHT 6ft (1.8m)

SPREAD 18in (45cm)

SITE Full sun

SOIL Free-draining

HARDINESS Z6–9 H9–6

FLOWERING Summer

Fragaria 'Pink Panda' Strawberry

F

THIS IS NOT A FRUITING STRAWBERRY—there are better, more prolific alternatives with sweeter fruit. Rather, it is an ornamental, clump-forming, spreading plant with fresh green leaves and pink flowers. 'Pink Panda' makes an attractive edging plant, or it can be grown in gaps in a terrace or patio. New, young plants are attached to the parent by what looks like an umbilical cord—once the new plants are growing well, simply snip the cord and move them to your preferred position in the garden. If it becomes too invasive, clumps can be easily removed.

OTHER VARIETY *F. vesca* 'Variegata' (gray-green leaves with creamy white markings).

PLANT PROFILE

HEIGHT 4–6in (10–15cm)

SPREAD 4–6in (10–15cm)

SITE Full sun or light dappled shade

SOIL Average, free-draining

HARDINESS Z5–9 H9–5

FLOWERING Late spring to midautumn

F

Francoa sonchifolia Bridal wreath

THIS IS A HIGHLY ATTRACTIVE, intriguing plant. It makes rosettes of hairy, crinkled, bright green leaves that hug the ground, and sends up vertical spikes of tiny, pure pink flowers in midsummer. The flowers stay fresh for a long time, giving a beautiful border display. It needs free-draining soil because the roots will quickly rot if stuck in cold, wet, winter soil. And in colder zones, it also needs a warm, sunny situation. The best way to increase your stock of plants is to divide them in the spring—make sure that new plants are well watered until they are firmly rooted and established.

OTHER VARIETIES *F. appendiculata* (pale pink flowers); *F. ramosa* (white flowers with pink markings).

PLANT PROFILE

HEIGHT 30in (75cm)

SPREAD 18in (45cm)

SITE Full sun or partial shade

SOIL Free-draining

HARDINESS Z7–9 H9–7

FLOWERING Midsummer

Gaillardia 'Kobold' Blanket flower

G

THE FLAMBOYANT, EXTRA LARGE, daisylike flowers of this plant add fizz to any border. The round blooms have a prominent red disk in the middle, and the petals are red with yellow tips. Blanket flowers need average (not too rich), free-draining soil, and are reasonably drought-tolerant. The stems are quite floppy, however, and need to be supported by twiggy sticks so that the colorful petals are clearly visible. The blooms are good for cutting and will enliven any indoor display. Alternatives include 'Dazzler' and 'Wirral Flame' which are orange-red with yellow tips, and the wine-red 'Burgunder'.

OTHER VARIETY *G.* x *grandiflora* (taller-growing, flowers with yellow and red petals and yellow-brown centers).

PLANT PROFILE
HEIGHT 12in (30cm)
SPREAD 18in (45cm)
SITE Full sun
SOIL Average, free-draining
HARDINESS Z3–8 H8–1
FLOWERING Early summer to early autumn

G

Galega officinalis Goat's rue

A COTTAGE GARDEN FAVORITE, goat's rue forms a spread of pealike flowers on scores of floppy spikes that require staking for a good display. Use it in borders to link different color schemes, or to contrast with more upright, architectural plants. If growing the mauve form, it is worth mixing it with the white 'Alba'. Plants spread by seed, soon forming large clumps (to prevent this, nip off the fading flowers before they set seed). Quite unfussy, it will grow in most soils, from moist to dry, and tolerates light shade.

OTHER VARIETIES *G.* x *hartlandii* 'Lady Wilson' (bicolored mauve-blue and white flowers); *G. orientalis* (blue-violet flowers).

PLANT PROFILE
HEIGHT 1–5ft (30cm–1.5m)
SPREAD 3ft (1m)
SITE Full sun or partial shade
SOIL Average
HARDINESS Z5–10
FLOWERING Mid- and late summer

Galium odoratum Sweet woodruff

G

GIVEN PLENTY OF SUN at the edge of a wooded area, this attractive little plant will spread freely. The tiny flowers perch above bright green leaves and, after two or three years, it will make a beautiful ground-covering carpet. Ideally, the soil needs to be on the moist side and fertile. To increase your stock of new plants, divide and replant clumps in the early spring. Beware of planting sweet woodruff in borders because, although pretty, it is quite invasive and soon becomes a nuisance.

OTHER VARIETY *G. verum* (narrow leaves, yellow flowers).

PLANT PROFILE
HEIGHT 18in (45cm)
SPREAD 18in (45cm)
SITE Sun or partial shade
SOIL Moist, fertile
HARDINESS Z5–8 H8–5
FLOWERING Late spring to midsummer

G | *Gaura lindheimeri* Bee blossom

FROM A DISTANCE THE SMALL, WHITE, long-lasting flowers on top of the slender stems look like butterflies. Gaura is a bonus in formal borders and cottage gardens, where it doesn't need copious watering in prolonged dry periods yet still performs well. Its "fluttery" flowers and small leaves soften the scene when planted near a chunky shrub or a dominating feature. While small gardens are unlikely to need more than one plant, if you want more, it is very easy to propagate in the spring, whether by cuttings or division.

OTHER VARIETIES *G. lindheimeri* 'Corrie's Gold' (gold-margined leaves); *G. lindheimeri* 'Siskiyou Pink' (warm pink flowers); *G. lindheimeri* 'Whirling Butterflies' (smaller-growing, gray-green leaves, red flowers).

PLANT PROFILE

HEIGHT To 5ft (1.5m)

SPREAD 3ft (1m)

SITE Full sun

SOIL Free-draining

HARDINESS Z6–8 H9–6

FLOWERING Late spring to early autumn

Gentiana asclepiadea Willow gentian

IN ORDER TO SEE a good display of the 2in- (5cm-) long flowers, you must cater to the needs of this plant. The soil must be moist and rich, and mulched in spring with a thick layer of leaf mold. Plant the willow gentian on the shady side of a shrub or in light shade in a border. When it is growing well, the flower stems tend to arch over, adding an informal note. Try to pick the right site to start with because established plants dislike being moved. Shorter gentians, such as *Gentiana acaulis*, are good for the rock garden.

OTHER VARIETIES *G. asclepiadea* var. *alba* (green-tinged white flowers); *G.* 'Inverleith' (smaller-growing, intense pale blue flowers with darker stripes); *G. septemfida* (purplish blue flowers).

PLANT PROFILE

HEIGHT 24–36in (60–90cm)

SPREAD 18in (45cm)

SITE Light shade

SOIL Moist, fertile

HARDINESS Z6–9 H9–6

FLOWERING Mid- or late summer to early autumn

G | *Geranium* 'Johnson's Blue'

JUSTIFIABLY A BIG FAVORITE, this perennial produces a prolific display of saucer-shaped, lavender-blue flowers that lend themselves to all sorts of of color contrasts. As with any any blue flower, when it is seen in light shade the blue looks slightly darker than when in full sun. After it is finished flowering, shear the plant to produce a fresh, neat clump of leaves. Geraniums grow in most soils, except for extremes of dry and wet, and in sun or shade. There are also dozens of varieties to choose from in the white-pink-purple-blue range.

OTHER VARIETIES G. 'Ann Folkard' (magenta flowers veined with black); *G. cinereum* 'Ballerina' (purplish red flowers with darker veins).

PLANT PROFILE
HEIGHT 12–18in (30–45cm)
SPREAD 24–30in (60–75cm)
SITE Full sun or partial shade
SOIL Average, free-draining
HARDINESS Z4–8 H8–1
FLOWERING Summer

DOWNY MILDEW

Pale yellow or light brown leaf discoloration and off-white fungal patches beneath the foliage are both signs of this disease. Remove all affected leaves promptly and spray upper and lower surfaces of others with a fungicide containing mancozeb.

Geranium himalayense 'Plenum'

G

THIS LOW-GROWING GERANIUM has its main flush of violet-blue blooms—set against deeply cut, distinctively veined foliage—in early summer. Use its spreading, scrambling growth to your advantage, letting it tumble over the edges of a straight path to soften and blur its line, or grow it beneath roses and in front of shrubs, where it will swamp any weeds. Geraniums are happy in most soils except for extremes of dry and wet, and will grow in full sun or shade.

OTHER VARIETIES *G. clarkei* 'Kashmir White' (white flowers with lilac-pink veins); *G. himalayense* 'Gravetye' (blue flowers shading into red at the center); *G. renardii* (white to lavender flowers with violet veins).

PLANT PROFILE

HEIGHT 10in (25cm)

SPREAD 24in (60cm)

SITE Full sun or partial shade

SOIL Average, free-draining

HARDINESS Z4–7 H7–1

FLOWERING Early summer

G | *Geranium sanguineum* Bloody cranesbill

THE COMMON NAME HERE comes from the fantastic clash of orange-, red-, and brown-tinted autumn foliage. The bloody cranesbill flowers over a long summer period, forming mats of deeply divided foliage and pretty, cup-shaped, magenta-pink flowers. Grow this plant in rock and gravel gardens, gaps in paving, or as groundcover. It also makes a good edging for the front of a border or to line a pathway. Geraniums grow in most soils except for extremes of dry and wet, and are happy in sun or light shade.

OTHER VARIETIES *G. sanguineum* 'Album' (white flowers); *G. sanguineum* 'Elsbeth' (bright purple flowers); *G. sanguineum* 'Glenluce' (rose pink flowers); *G. sanguineum* 'Max Frei' (magenta flowers).

PLANT PROFILE
HEIGHT 8in (20cm)
SPREAD 16in (40cm)
SITE Sun or light shade
SOIL Average, free-draining
HARDINESS Z3–8 H8–1
FLOWERING Summer

Geum 'Lady Stratheden' Avens

G

RELIABLY UPBEAT AND CHEERFUL, 'Lady Stratheden' flowers over an extended period from late spring, and mixes well with the bright red of *Geum* 'Mrs. J. Bradshaw', sometimes known as 'Fireball'. Use geums in conjunction with shrubs that have a shorter flowering period—perhaps the spring-flowering *Choisya ternata*—where they will provide a continuity of color throughout the summer. Geums are happy in most soils apart from heavy, waterlogged clay; good drainage is an important factor, as is bright sun.

OTHER VARIETIES G. 'Coppertone' (smaller-growing, apricot flowers with red centers); G. 'Fire Opal' (taller-growing, semidouble, dark orange flowers); G. 'Lemon Drops' (smaller-growing, lemon yellow flowers).

PLANT PROFILE

HEIGHT 16–24in (40–60cm)

SPREAD 24in (60cm)

SITE Full sun

SOIL Average, free-draining

HARDINESS Z5–9 H9–5

FLOWERING Late spring to summer

G | *Gillenia trifoliata* Bowman's root

A GENTLE SHOW OF PINKISH WHITE FLOWERS appears in early summer, with each bloom looking like a butterfly that has just landed on top of a red-tinted stem. The color is enlivened by the red calyces (leaflike structures at the base of the flower) and red autumn foliage. Bowman's root is an excellent addition to any border with slightly acidic or even neutral soil that is moist but free-draining. It likes a bright position in the garden, but some shade is needed during the hottest part of the day. To increase your stock of plants, divide it in early spring or midautumn and immediately replant the new sections.

PLANT PROFILE

HEIGHT To 3ft (1m)

SPREAD 24in (60cm)

SITE Partial shade

SOIL Moist, free-draining

HARDINESS Z5–9 H9–5

FLOWERING Early summer

Gladiolus communis subsp. *byzantinus*

G

USEFUL IN ALL TYPES OF BORDERS, this hardy plant produces a shock of magenta blooms in early summer that immediately grabs your attention. It has a brief flowering spell and should be positioned where other perennials can take over and hide its fading foliage later in the year. It grows best in soil with good drainage and needs the protection of a covering of mulch in winter. Other varieties need very sheltered sites, or they can be potted and kept somewhere frost-free over the winter.

OTHER VARIETIES *G. callianthus* (white flowers, with purple-marked throats, in late summer); *G. cardinalis* (bright red flowers with a white flash); *G. tristis* (taller-growing, yellow or creamy white flowers).

PLANT PROFILE
HEIGHT To 3ft (1m)
SPREAD 3in (8cm)
SITE Full sun
SOIL Free-draining
HARDINESS Z8–10 H9–1
FLOWERING Late spring to early summer

G | *Glaucidium palmatum* Shirane-aoi

THIS HIGHLY UNDERRATED, slow-growing, mauve-flowering plant is suitable for shady sites, such as you might find in a woodland garden or at the shady end of a border. It produces an attractive mix of light green crinkled leaves, about 8in (20cm) long, with jagged edges, and 3in- (8cm-) wide flowers with golden centers. Grow this plant in rich, cool, moist ground where there is shelter from winds that could damage its leaves. Beware of slug attacks in the spring that could mar the new season's growth.

OTHER VARIETY *G. palmatum* var. *leucanthum* (white flowers).

PLANT PROFILE
HEIGHT 18in (45cm)
SPREAD 18in (45cm)
SITE Partial to deep shade
SOIL Moist, fertile
HARDINESS Z6–9 H9–6
FLOWERING Late spring and early summer

Glaucium flavum Yellow horned poppy

G

AN EYE-CATCHING PERENNIAL that looks particularly fine when set against the stony ground of a gravel garden. The rosettes of large, almost cabbagelike, fleshy leaves are blue-green with wavy margins. Although short-lived, it self-seeds readily, especially when grown on free-draining, average-to-poor soil. It can just about be included in an herb garden because the ancient Greeks thought it could "purge the belly," while the leaves "removed ulcers from sheep's eyes."

OTHER VARIETIES *G. corniculatum* (smaller-growing, crimson-red to orange flowers); *G. grandiflorum* (smaller-growing, dark orange to crimson flowers).

PLANT PROFILE		
HEIGHT 12–36in (30–90cm)		
SPREAD To 18in (45cm)		
SITE Full sun		
SOIL Average, free-draining		
HARDINESS Z6–9 H9–6		
FLOWERING Summer		

Divide large plants like gunneras in the spring, before growth starts. Use two forks, back to back, to pry apart the main clump into more manageable sections.

G

Gunnera manicata Giant rhubarb

THIS IS THE TOP CHOICE if you are looking for a magnificent pond-side plant, but it definitely needs a large garden. Each spring, *Gunnera manicata* produces fantastic, near-vertical, prickly stems and thick, oval leathery leaves, which are the largest on any hardy plant, growing up to 6ft (2m) wide. It is also possible to stand up straight under a gunnera without your head touching the foliage. The tiny flowers are packed on strange, conelike structures under the leaves. The plant dies back in the autumn, when the leaves should be folded over the crown as protection. Provide moist soil and a sheltered site.

OTHER VARIETY *G. tinctoria* (smaller-growing, though still large).

PLANT PROFILE
HEIGHT 8ft (2.5m)
SPREAD 11ft (3.5m)
SITE Full sun or partial shade
SOIL Moist
HARDINESS Z7–11 H12–7
FLOWERING Early summer

Gypsophila 'Rosenschleier' Baby's breath

AIRY, OPEN SPRAYS of tiny white flowers (quickly turning pale pink) give this plant its other name of 'Rosy Veil'. Unlike the taller gypsophilas, it needs to be grown at the front of a border, where it forms a dense mound of semievergreen leaves. Plant it on light, free-draining soil, and choose the right planting place to start with, because it dislikes disturbance. An alternative short gypsophila with pale pink flowers is *Gypsophila repens* 'Dorothy Teacher'.

OTHER VARIETIES   *G. cerastioides* (smaller-growing, white flowers); *G. paniculata* 'Bristol Fairy' (taller-growing, double white flowers); *G. paniculata* 'Compacta Plena' (double, soft pink to white flowers).

PLANT PROFILE
HEIGHT 16–20in (40–50cm)
SPREAD 3ft (1m)
SITE Full sun
SOIL Free-draining
HARDINESS Z4–9 H9–3
FLOWERING Mid- and late summer

H | *Hacquetia epipactis*

THIS FUN, QUIRKY LITTLE PLANT is ideal for any moist, shady parts of the garden. The clusters of tiny yellow flowers, which gradually turn green, are surrounded by a ring of bright green, petal-like bracts, and these are followed soon after by the appearance of the oval leaves. *Hacquetia epipactis* can be grown in rock gardens, where its low mounds are ideal for the scale of planting. It also provides a good partner to plants such as hostas, which enjoy the same site and soil conditions. Look out for slugs and snails in spring, since they can quickly demolish the new growth.

PLANT PROFILE

HEIGHT 6in (15cm)

SPREAD 9in (23cm)

SITE Partial shade

SOIL Moist

HARDINESS Z5–7 H7–5

FLOWERING Late winter and early spring

Hakonechloa macra 'Aureola' Golden Japanese forest grass

THIS HIGH-PERFORMANCE GRASS is grown chiefly for its fountain of 10in- (25cm-) long, bright yellow- and green-striped leaves. It hits a high note from the moment the foliage starts to appear in spring; come autumn, the leaves take on a red tinge that persists into winter. 'Aureola' makes a satisfying oval shape, and can be used as a feature plant in a pot, to highlight the front of a border, or to fringe a pond. It can also be grown in rows, softening the edges of a path, and in formal, geometric gardens interspersed with clipped boxwood (*Buxus*) plants. The pale green flowers (*see inset*) appear from late summer to early autumn.

PLANT PROFILE
HEIGHT 14in (35cm)
SPREAD 16in (40cm)
SITE Full sun or partial shade
SOIL Moist, fertile, free-draining
HARDINESS Z5–9 H9–5
FLOWERING Late summer to midautumn

H

Hedychium densiflorum Ginger lily

SHOWY, SHAPELY, GLOSSY LEAVES, up to 16in (40cm) long and, in the summer, a short stem packed with tiny flowers radiating all the way around are the key features of this dramatic plant. Most gardens have a slightly shady, sheltered spot, with moist but free-draining soil, and that's all it takes to grow this richly scented Himalayan perennial. Without these conditions it can be grown in a large pot. An even showier alternative is the scented *Hedychium gardnerianum*.

OTHER VARIETIES *H. coccineum* (smaller-growing, pale to deep red, orange, pink, or white flowers); *H. densiflorum* 'Assam Orange' (densely borne, deep orange flowers).

PLANT PROFILE

HEIGHT To 15ft (5m)

SPREAD 6ft (2m)

SITE Sun or partial shade

SOIL Fertile, moist but free-draining

HARDINESS Z8–11 H12–8

FLOWERING Late summer

Helenium 'Moerheim Beauty' Sneezeweed

THESE KEY PLANTS for the summer border have an arresting show of large, daisylike, orange-red and yellow flowers. Those of 'Moerheim Beauty' have coppery red blooms and the typical, highly distinctive central eye—in this case, dark brown. It makes a perfect background plant for drifts of fiery reds and oranges, and its long flowering season extends from the start to the end of summer. Not too fussy, it will thrive in most soils with decent drainage, but not in dry, baked conditions. It is a sturdy grower and does not need staking.

OTHER VARIETIES *H.* 'Bruno' (taller-growing, deep crimson flowers); *H.* 'Goldfuchs' (tawny orange flowers); *H.* 'Wyndley' (yellow flowers overlaid with dark orange).

PLANT PROFILE	
HEIGHT 3ft (1m)	
SPREAD 24in (60cm)	
SITE Full sun	
SOIL Moist	
HARDINESS Z4–8 H8–1	
FLOWERING Early to late summer	

H

Helianthus 'Lemon Queen' Sunflower

NOT ALL SUNFLOWERS are giant annuals with satellite dish–sized, brash yellow heads—'Lemon Queen' has soft, pale yellow, small flowers, about 4in (10cm) wide, with a darker yellow eye. It is a bushy performer for late summer, with an abundant supply of blooms, but needs support to stop it from flopping. It adds a cheery touch to cottage gardens, and you can also grow a row of plants as an internal hedge, with clematis and nasturtiums sprinting through the stems. Provide fertile, moist but free-draining soil.

OTHER VARIETIES *H.* 'Capenoch Star' (lemon yellow flowers); *H.* 'Loddon Gold' (double, rich yellow flowers); *H.* 'Monarch' (semi-double, yellow-brown flowers); *H. salicifolius* (taller-growing, gold flowers).

PLANT PROFILE
HEIGHT 5½ft (1.7m)
SPREAD 4ft (1.2m)
SITE Full sun
SOIL Fertile, moist but free-draining
HARDINESS Z5–9 H9–5
FLOWERING Summer

Helichrysum 'Schwefellicht'

H

SMALL, FLUFFY, SULFUR YELLOW FLOWERS that turn orange-yellow, held on white, woolly stems, create an attractive display in late summer. This helichrysum can be grown at the front of a border, in raised beds, or in a Mediterranean-style or gravel garden, where it combines well with lavenders and the shorter varieties of red-hot poker (*Kniphofia*). Excellent drainage is vital for this plant to thrive, while the soil can vary from poor to average. Most of the good alternatives are shrubs, such as *Helichrysum petiolare* and *H. splendidum*, but there is a smaller white-flowering perennial available.

OTHER VARIETY *H. milfordiae* (smaller-growing, white flowers).

PLANT PROFILE	
HEIGHT 16in (40cm)	
SPREAD 12in (30cm)	
SITE Full sun	
SOIL Average, free-draining	
HARDINESS Z9–10 H10–9	
FLOWERING Late summer	

H | *Helictotrichon sempervirens* Blue oat grass

THE SUMMER-FLOWERING STEMS of this neat-looking, bristling grass shoot high above its near-vertical, narrow, gray-blue leaves. It is a beautiful, graceful plant when in bloom, and adds great charm to any gravel garden or border, where the tall flower stems will stand out best when set against a dark background. The soil needs to be free-draining and preferably on the poor side. Leave it unpruned over winter, and cut it back in the early spring. Comb out old, dead leaves with your splayed fingers, but beware of the sharp tips, which can cut your skin.

OTHER VARIETY *H. sempervirens* 'Saphirsprudel' (more vigorous, broader leaves).

PLANT PROFILE
HEIGHT To 4½ft (1.4m)
SPREAD 24in (60cm)
SITE Full sun
SOIL Poor, free-draining
HARDINESS Z4–9 H9–1
FLOWERING Early and midsummer

Heliopsis helianthoides var. *scabra* 'Sommersonne' Ox-eye

H

THE BRACING, GOLDEN YELLOW, daisylike flowers of the ox-eye last all through the summer. Sometimes known as the false sunflower because of the similarity in flower shape, it looks good when grown in drifts, but never plant it next to a gentle pastel color or it will hog the limelight. It requires minimum care, does not need regular feeding or watering, and thrives in most soils, even quite poor ones. It makes bushy clumps, but needs some support to keep the stems erect especially in exposed windy gardens.

OTHER VARIETIES   *H. helianthoides* var. *scabra* 'Goldgefieder' (taller-growing, double, golden yellow flowers); *H. helianthoides* var. *scabra* 'Goldgrünherz' (double, lemon yellow flowers).

PLANT PROFILE
HEIGHT 3ft (1m)
SPREAD 24in (60cm)
SITE Full sun
SOIL Average
HARDINESS Z4–9 H9–1
FLOWERING Midsummer to early autumn

LEAF BLOTCH

All hellebores are prone to this problem, in which gray-brown blotches are seen on leaves and stems. Remove all affected parts at once, and new leaves should soon regenerate.

H

Helleborus x *sternii* Hellebore

IT IS IMPOSSIBLE TO TELL which of its parents this hellebore will most resemble. It can look more like the hardy *Helleborus argutifolius*, with its tough, toothed leaves and white flowers, or the smaller *H. lividus*, with pink-flushed blooms. Either way, it is trouble-free and generally has pinkish purple flushed flowers. The two best-known types are 'Boughton Beauty' (often closer to *H. argutifolius*), which has greenish flowers, pinkish purple on the outside, and 'Blackthorn' (smaller, like *H. lividus*), with pink-tinged green flowers and unusual veined foliage. Both need shelter from cold winds.

OTHER VARIETIES *H. foetidus* (taller, purple-edged green flowers); *H. niger* (white, or pink-flushed flowers, on purple-marked stems).

PLANT PROFILE

HEIGHT 12–14in (30–35cm)

SPREAD 12in (30cm)

SITE Full sun or dappled shade

SOIL Moist, free-draining

HARDINESS Z6–9 H9–6

FLOWERING Late winter to midspring

Hemerocallis 'Stafford' Daylily

H

WITH A REGULAR SUCCESSION of flowers, each lasting a day, 'Stafford' is a typical daylily. It has enormous possibilities in the border, adding color when early summer performers take a rest, or in a lively plan with bright, hot colors. Daylilies need fertile, moist soil with plenty of well-rotted compost in the spring. Plants must be kept well watered from spring onward, and perform well in a sunny site. There are scores of daylilies available, in colors ranging from white to yellow, orange, lavender-blue, purple, and rich, dark red.

OTHER VARIETIES *H.* 'Green Flutter' (light yellow flowers with green-tinted throats); *H.* 'Stella de Oro' (bright yellow flowers).

PLANT PROFILE
HEIGHT 28in (70cm)
SPREAD 3ft (1m)
SITE Full sun
SOIL Moist, fertile
HARDINESS Z3–10 H12–2
FLOWERING Midsummer

Hepatica nobilis Liverwort

TYPICALLY GROWN BENEATH TREES, on the shady side of a shrub, or in pots in shady corners, this plant is an attractive addition to the spring garden. The open blue flowers, held above the leaves on top of thin stalks, may even start to bloom in late winter. Choose the right position from the outset because it dislikes being moved once in the ground. The soil must be rich and moist, the heavier the better, but not boggy. You can divide clumps in spring, but the divisions tend to take their time to become fully established.

OTHER VARIETIES *H. acutiloba* (smaller-growing, blue, pink, or white flowers); *H. x media* 'Ballardii' (taller-growing, deep blue flowers); *H. transsilvanica* (taller-growing, blue, white, or pale pink flowers).

PLANT PROFILE
HEIGHT 4in (10cm)
SPREAD 6in (15cm)
SITE Partial shade
SOIL Fertile, moist but free-draining
HARDINESS Z5–8 H8–4
FLOWERING Early spring

Hesperis matronalis var. *albiflora* Sweet rocket

H

THIS ESSENTIAL, EASYGOING, and sweetly scented (especially in the evening) plant adds a quiet, gentle, unforced touch to the late-spring garden. It should be grown with the lilac or purple kinds (*Hesperis matronalis*), and planted among spring-flowering shrubs or bulbs for a colorful, perfumed display. Although short-lived, rarely surviving more than three years, it self-seeds prolifically. Look for seedlings close to the parent plant in the spring, and move them to other sites in the garden. Dappled shade and poor soil are the basic requirements.

OTHER VARIETIES *H. matronalis* (lilac or purple flowers); *H. matronalis* var. *albiflora* 'Alba Plena' (double white flowers).

PLANT PROFILE
HEIGHT 3ft (1m)
SPREAD 18in (45cm)
SITE Sun or partial shade
SOIL Poor, free-draining
HARDINESS Z4–9 H9–1
FLOWERING Late spring to midsummer

H | *Heuchera* 'Chocolate Ruffles'

THE NEW HEUCHERAS have highly attractive winter leaves—those of 'Chocolate Ruffles', for example, are rich brown and purple beneath with ruffled edges. The small, purplish flowers are held on thin, bare stems, giving an airy, dainty appearance. Other good choices include 'Pewter Moon', with silver markings on the leaves and pale pink flowers, and *Heuchera micrantha* var. *diversifolia* 'Palace Purple', with bronze-red, jagged-edged foliage and greenish cream flowers. All like rich, moist but free-draining soil, and a sunny or shaded site.

OTHER VARIETIES *H.* 'Cascade Dawn' (red-purple leaves with pewter markings); *H.* 'Red Spangles' (smaller-growing, scarlet-crimson flowers throughout summer).

PLANT PROFILE
HEIGHT 30in (75cm)
SPREAD 16in (40cm)
SITE Sun or light shade
SOIL Moist, fertile, free-draining
HARDINESS Z4–9
FLOWERING Early summer

x *Heucherella alba* 'Bridget Bloom'

H

LUSH, EVERGREEN, LOBED FOLIAGE for cottage gardens and borders is the key attraction of this plant. It has airy sprays of tiny pink and white flowers held on slim spires above the leaves. The foliage grows to 4in (10cm) long, and initially has brown marbling, turning bronze in the autumn. For the best results, provide partial shade and free-draining soil, which can be slightly acidic. 'Bridget Bloom' combines well with asters, white geraniums, and heucheras.

OTHER VARIETIES x *H. alba* 'Rosalie' (veined green leaves with a darker center and pink flowers); x *H. tiarelloides* (larger-growing, tiny pink flowers on brownish red stems from midspring to early summer).

PLANT PROFILE

HEIGHT To 16in (40cm)

SPREAD 12in (30cm)

SITE Sun or partial shade

SOIL Fertile, free-draining

HARDINESS Z5–8 H8–5

FLOWERING Late spring to midautumn

H

Hordeum jubatum Squirrel tail grass

THIS BEAUTIFUL SMALL GRASS has silky, silvery plumes, often tinged with purple at the top, that sway gracefully when caught by even the slightest breeze. Toward the end of summer, the plumes turn beige. This versatile grass can be used in all kinds of ways—ideas include planting it *en masse* to cover a small bed, with several strategically placed feature plants rising out of it, or using it to edge the front of a border. Although *Hordeum jubatum* is extremely short-lived, this is not a problem because it is a prolific self-seeder. In the spring, delay weeding—what look like small clumps of lawn grass in the border may, in fact, be young plants.

PLANT PROFILE
HEIGHT 20in (50cm)
SPREAD 12in (30cm)
SITE Full sun
SOIL Fertile, free-draining
HARDINESS Z4–8 H8–1
FLOWERING Early and midsummer

DIVISION

To divide a large hosta clump, use a spade to cut through the tough rootstock. Each division should have a few good buds. Then use a clean, sharp knife to remove any damaged tissue.

Hosta undulata var. *albomarginata*

H

THIS LARGE, SHOWY HOSTA has 7in- (18cm-) long leaves, each with a distinct white rim, and funnel-shaped mauve summer flowers on tall stems. It is an excellent plant for a damp, shady site and is a good performer in a border or in an attractive, large pot. This is just one of a huge variety of hostas that range in color from yellow-green leaves ('September Sun') or bluish leaves ('Halcyon'), to those with flashy white margins ('Francee'). All hostas can suffer badly from slug damage, so take precautions—piling sharp sand around the stems may deter them, and it also helps to highlight the foliage.

OTHER VARIETIES *H*. 'Frances Williams' (blue-green leaves, wide green-yellow margins); *H*. 'Patriot' (olive green leaves, white margins).

PLANT PROFILE	
HEIGHT 22in (55cm)	
SPREAD 3ft (1m)	
SITE Full or partial shade	
SOIL Moist, fertile	
HARDINESS Z3–9 H9–1	
FLOWERING Summer	

H | *Houttuynia cordata* 'Chameleon' Chameleon plant

DAMP, SHADY PLACES in the eastern Asia are home to the parent of this plant—precisely the same conditions that 'Chameleon' needs in the garden. Its neatly marked leaves have patches of dark pinky red, green, and cream, but it needs bright light rather than shade for the coloring to become really vivid. It is tempting to plant it in the border, but do so at your peril—it's a notorious invader and is far better used as groundcover. Insert paving slabs or slate vertically around the walls of its planting hole, creating a lined square or rectangular pit, to curtail its spreading roots.

OTHER VARIETY *H. cordata* 'Flore Pleno' (leaves variegated in green, pale yellow, and red, flowers surrounded by white bracts).

PLANT PROFILE

HEIGHT To 12in (30cm)

SPREAD Indefinite

SITE Full sun or dappled shade

SOIL Moist

HARDINESS Z5–11 H12–1

FLOWERING Spring

Hypericum perforatum St. John's wort

H

USED BY HERBALISTS FOR CENTURIES, this plant justifies its presence merely by producing its bright yellow flowers in a border or herb garden with average soil. A multipurpose herb, it oozes an antidepressant red dye when mixed with alcohol, and a yellow dye when mixed with alum. Medicinally, it is said to cure just about everything—from burns and tennis elbow to shingles and sciatica—and it's often used in oils and tinctures. Use it only with professional guidance, however; eating it can cause a variety of severe effects, particularly lesions on white skin when exposed to sunlight. The word "wort" originally meant root, herb, or plant.

OTHER VARIETY *H. orientale* (smaller-growing, golden yellow flowers).

PLANT PROFILE
HEIGHT 24–42in (60–110cm)
SPREAD To 24in (60cm)
SITE Full sun
SOIL Average, free-draining
HARDINESS Z3–8 H8–1
FLOWERING Midsummer to midautumn

I *Imperata cylindrica* 'Rubra' Japanese blood grass

HARD TO IGNORE, this flashy grass starts off red at the tip and then slowly "burns" down until virtually the whole blade is a rich red color. The silvery flowers make a good contrast with the foliage, but they appear only in long, hot summers. It can be used in a wide range of situations: at the front of a border, edging paths, around artificial ponds, and, for a shocking contrast, in a white-themed garden. Unfortunately, it dies back in winter, when it needs cutting to the ground and, because it is on the tender side, a thick winter mulch of compost to protect the roots. This warning is particularly relevant to young plants. It hates wet soil, and will flourish when growing in free-draining conditions in sun or light shade.

PLANT PROFILE

HEIGHT 16in (40cm)

SPREAD 12in (30cm)

SITE Sun or light shade

SOIL Fertile, free-draining

HARDINESS Z5–9 H9–3

FLOWERING Late summer

Incarvillea delavayi Hardy gloxinia

I

REMARKABLY EXOTIC YET EASY TO GROW, the rich-colored flower trumpets of this plant have a yellow throat and are borne on top of erect stems, well clear of the leaves at the base. It likes free-draining, fertile soil that does not bake dry over summer. Because it hates sitting in soaking wet soil, plant it just under the soil surface and protect it over winter with a thick mulch of compost. The exotic flowers make it tempting to try growing other incarvilleas, but this one is the most popular because it is so reliable.

OTHER VARIETY *I. mairei* (purple-crimson flowers with white-striped purple on the lower lobes).

PLANT PROFILE
HEIGHT 24in (60cm)
SPREAD 12in (30cm)
SITE Full sun, light shade
SOIL Fertile, free-draining
HARDINESS Z6–10 H9–3
FLOWERING Early and midsummer

Inula hookeri

THIS HARDY DAISY IS A ROBUST PLANT, with pale yellow flowers, up to 3in (8cm) wide, the spidery petals of which shoot out from the inner brownish yellow disk. The whole plant can be slightly invasive in ideal conditions, but the roots are easily sliced with a spade and the excess growth dug out. If space permits, try *Inula magnifica*, which is the largest species available, growing up to 6ft (2m) high and 3ft (1m) wide. The flowers are golden yellow, and it definitely needs a place at the back of a border.

OTHER VARIETIES *I. ensifolia* (smaller-growing, golden yellow flowers); *I. helenium* (taller-growing, bright yellow flowers); *I. orientalis* (orange-yellow flowers); *I. racemosa* (taller-growing, light yellow flowers).

PLANT PROFILE

HEIGHT 24–30in (60–75cm)

SPREAD 24in (60cm)

SITE Partial shade

SOIL Moist, fertile, free-draining

HARDINESS Z4–8 H8–1

FLOWERING Late summer to midautumn

Iris pallida 'Variegata'

With its semievergreen leaves thrusting out of the soil like swords, this is a first-rate, highly versatile, spreading border iris. The foliage is bright green with a golden yellow stripe, and the plant makes a strong architectural statement. The late spring and early summer flowers are soft blue. Use it to line a path, or in a border or gravel garden interspersed with tall alliums or late-flowering tulips. *Iris pallida* 'Argentea Variegata' is equally attractive, though less vigorous, with silvery white-striped leaves. Both irises need free-draining soil and a sunny situation to thrive.

OTHER VARIETY *I. laevigata* 'Variegata' (smaller-growing, pale purple-blue flowers in summer, white- and green-striped leaves).

PLANT PROFILE
HEIGHT To 4ft (1.2m)
SPREAD Indefinite
SITE Sun
SOIL Fertile, free-draining
HARDINESS Z3–9 H9–1
FLOWERING Late spring and early summer

K | *Knautia macedonica* Macedonian scabious

WITH ITS LONG, THIN, WIRY STEMS and small, roundish, dark red pincushion flowers on top, this plant always catches the eye. It is more of a combination plant than a feature, and needs to be placed where the flowers stand out against, and poke through, the yellows and whites of adjacent plants. These neighbors should also provide some support for its floppy stems; if they're not suitable, push in twiggy sticks to prop up the plant. *Knautia macedonica* will survive in heavy soil but prefers free-draining ground. Further plants can be raised easily from cuttings taken in the spring.

OTHER VARIETY *K. arvensis* (taller-growing, bluish lilac, flat-topped flowers, dull green leaves).

PLANT PROFILE

HEIGHT To 32in (80cm)

SPREAD 18in (45cm)

SITE Full sun

SOIL Free-draining

HARDINESS Z5–9 H9–5

FLOWERING Mid- and late summer

Kniphofia triangularis Red-hot poker

K

EVERY GARDEN NEEDS a group of these clump-forming red-hot pokers. The plant has clublike stems packed with tiny flowers at the top. *Kniphofia triangularis* is excellent in lively gravel gardens and end-of-season borders with asters, dahlias, fuchsias, hedychiums, and rudbeckias. Other flashy choices include the bright red 'Erecta', 'Mount Etna' (with scarlet buds and greenish yellow flowers), *K. rooperi* (with orange-red flowers turning orange-yellow), and scarlet 'Samuel's Sensation'. Plant them in moist but free-draining soil.

OTHER VARIETIES *K. caulescens* (taller-growing, coral-red flowers fading to pale yellow); *K.* 'Little Maid' (smaller-growing, pale yellow flowers); *K.* 'Sunningdale Yellow' (long-lasting yellow flowers).

PLANT PROFILE

HEIGHT 24–36in (60–90cm)

SPREAD 18in (45cm)

SITE Sun or partial shade

SOIL Fertile, moist but free-draining

HARDINESS Z4–9

FLOWERING Early and midautumn

Koeleria glauca Glaucous hair grass

GROWING IN THE WILD on sandy soil in Europe and Asia, glaucous hair grass makes a semievergreen upright clump with 8in- (20cm-) long, blue-tinged, gray-green leaves. The flowers appear slightly earlier than on many grasses. It is a valuable ingredient in a gravel garden, and makes an interesting edge to a border. Plant it in soil with excellent drainage. Because it declines in vigor in just a few growing seasons, you should dig up clumps and divide them every two years in the spring. Save the younger, more vigorous outer sections for replanting.

OTHER VARIETY *K. macrantha* (green foliage).

PLANT PROFILE
HEIGHT To 16in (40cm)
SPREAD 12in (30cm)
SITE Full sun or light shade
SOIL Free-draining
HARDINESS Z6–9
FLOWERING Early and midsummer

Lamium maculatum 'White Nancy' Deadnettle

LOW-GROWING AND SEMIEVERGREEN, this groundcover plant spreads vigorously. The tiny silver leaves have a green rim, and the nettlelike flowers are small and bright white. It makes excellent groundcover for shady sites, or use it to decorate winter containers on a sheltered patio. Other types produce pink, purple, and red flowers. The best noninvasive deadnettles are the pink to white *Lamium armenum*, and the 24in- (60cm-) high, pinkish purple *L. orvala*.

OTHER VARIETIES *L. maculatum* 'Aureum' (pink flowers, yellow leaves with paler centers); *L. maculatum* 'Beacon Silver' (pale pink flowers, green-margined silver leaves); *L. maculatum* 'Red Nancy' (purplish red flowers); *L. orvala* 'Album' (taller-growing, pinkish purple flowers).

PLANT PROFILE

HEIGHT 6in (15cm)

SPREAD To 3ft (1m) or more

SITE Partial or deep shade

SOIL Moist, free-draining

HARDINESS Z4–8 H8–1

FLOWERING Summer

Lathyrus vernus 'Alboroseus' Spring vetchling

TYPICALLY GROWN AT THE FRONT of a border, in rock gardens, or even in woodland areas, spring vetchling is used for its early pink and white flowers (unlike *Lathyrus vernus*, which has purple flowers). It produces dense growth with upright stems and lush green foliage, and needs free-draining soil, although it's perfectly happy in poor ground. However, it dislikes being dug up and planted in new sites, so try to find the right position from the start. For climbing, scented, annual sweet peas, look for varieties of *L. odoratus*.

OTHER VARIETY *L. aureus* (taller-growing, yellow-orange flowers from late spring to early summer, dark green leaves).

PLANT PROFILE

HEIGHT 8–18in (20–45cm)

SPREAD 18in (45cm)

SITE Full sun or light shade

SOIL Free-draining

HARDINESS Z5–7 H7–5

FLOWERING Spring

Lavatera maritima Mallow

L

GIVING A SUBTLE END-OF-SEASON SHOW, this form of perennial mallow produces pink, lilac-pink, or even white flowers, 1in (2.5cm) wide. The growth is upright and quite shrubby, leading some to regard it as a shrub. Plant it in free-draining soil and provide some shelter from the damaging effects of icy winds. It thrives in coastal gardens, where it is reliably evergreen. There are many other excellent mallows for midsummer flowers, including the perennial 'Bressingham Pink' and the shrubby, red-eyed, white 'Barnsley'.

OTHER VARIETIES *L. cachemiriana* (taller-growing, rose pink flowers); *L.* x *clementii* 'Shorty' (smaller-growing, white or rose pink flowers); *L. thuringiaca* (taller-growing, purple-pink flowers).

PLANT PROFILE	
HEIGHT 5ft (1.5m)	
SPREAD 3ft (1m)	
SITE Full sun	
SOIL Free-draining	
HARDINESS Z6–8 H9–7	
FLOWERING Late summer to midautumn	

L   *Lespedeza thunbergii* Bush clover

THIS SURPRISINGLY UNDERRATED plant provides an eye-catching contrast when planted with big, bold dahlias. It has delicate, small, beautifully formed purple-pink flowers on arching stems, and the leaves are small and oval. The display does not last that long—about two weeks—but the bush clover is worth including in a bed or border, since there is little else in early autumn quite like it. Provide light, free-draining soil; in heavier clay, growth will be much slower. Despite its shrubby appearance, it doesn't need pruning because winter frosts will cut it back, although it reliably reshoots from soil level the following spring.

OTHER VARIETY   *L. bicolor* (purple-pink flowers).

PLANT PROFILE	
HEIGHT 6ft (2m)	
SPREAD 10ft (3m)	
SITE Full sun	
SOIL Free-draining	
HARDINESS Z4–7 H7–1	
FLOWERING Early autumn	

Leucanthemum x *superbum* 'Wirral Supreme' Shasta daisy

EACH SUMMER THE SHASTA DAISIES can be relied on to give a good show. Robust and clump-forming, they have flowers with an outer ring of petals and a central eye. The blooms of 'Wirral Supreme' have a yellow eye, with a double row of white petals, and are held on long, thin stems above dark green leaves. For a slightly more eccentric display, try 'Phyllis Smith', which has long, thin, twisted petals. Both may need staking, and will thrive in sun or a little shade in gardens with moist but free-draining soil.

OTHER VARIETIES *L.* x *superbum* 'Aglaia' (shorter, with semidouble white flowers); *L.* x *superbum* 'Esther Read' (double white flowers); *L.* x *superbum* 'Silberprinzesschen' (shorter, with single white flowers).

PLANT PROFILE
HEIGHT 30in (75cm)
SPREAD 30in (75cm)
SITE Full sun or partial shade
SOIL Moist but free-draining
HARDINESS Z5–8 H8–5
FLOWERING Early summer to early autumn

L

Leymus arenarius Lyme grass

IN THE WILD IN NORTHERN EUROPE this grass is used to bind and
stabilize sand dunes, but its chief value in gardens is its blue-gray,
24in- (60cm-) high leaves. Cut back the foliage after flowering and
you will be rewarded with a fresh flush of colorful leaves to give
a strong show in the autumn. Plant lyme grass in free-draining soil
that's on the poor side. When happy, this drought-tolerant plant is
a robust spreader, but it can be contained by planting it in a spacious
hole lined with paving slabs. After a few years, the clump will need
to be dug up, thinned out, and replanted. The long, thin, graceful,
blue-gray flower spikes can be used in displays of cut flowers.

PLANT PROFILE

HEIGHT 5ft (1.5m)

SPREAD Indefinite

SITE Full sun

SOIL Poor, free-draining

HARDINESS Z4–10 H10–1

FLOWERING Summer

Liatris spicata Gayfeather

L

THIS LATE-SUMMER PLANT is useful for a hot spot in a border with moist but free-draining soil. Its stems stand smartly upright, at about shoulder-height, and are covered with clusters of tiny pink-purple or white flowers that open and fade gradually in succession from top to bottom. Other types offer various colors: 'Snow Queen' and 'Floristan Weiss' (white), 'Blue Bird' (blue-purple), and 'Kobold' (deep purple). Avoid growing gayfeather in heavy, water-retentive clay or it will die in its first winter.

OTHER VARIETY *L. pycnostachya* (bright purple flowers in dense spikes from midsummer).

PLANT PROFILE
HEIGHT 5ft (1.5m)
SPREAD 18in (45cm)
SITE Full sun
SOIL Moist but free-draining
HARDINESS Z4–9 H9–5
FLOWERING Late summer and early autumn

L | *Libertia grandiflora* New Zealand satin flower

ADDING INTEREST TO LATE-SPRING GARDENS, this evergreen, clump-forming plant sends up stems covered with sprays of small, white flowers above strap-shaped foliage that can reach 30in (75cm) in length. *Libertia formosa* is very similar and is a good alternative plant. Both are borderline hardy and need a thick, protective mulch of compost over winter, especially in their first few years, until they're well established. As an option, you can plant them in a sheltered, warm site—for example, at the base of a sunny wall. Rich, moist soil with good drainage is required.

OTHER VARIETIES *L. caerulescens* (smaller-growing, pale blue flowers); *L. ixioides* (smaller-growing, white flowers with brown or green).

PLANT PROFILE

HEIGHT To 3ft (1m)

SPREAD 24in (60cm)

SITE Full sun

SOIL Moist, fertile, free-draining

HARDINESS Z8–11 H12–8

FLOWERING Late spring and early summer

Ligularia dentata 'Desdemona' Golden groundsel

L

STRIKING AND IMMENSELY USEFUL, ligularias are suitable for slightly shady, fertile sites where the soil stays moist. If grown in sunnier sites, it needs copious watering in heatwave conditions to prevent the whole plant from suddenly collapsing. 'Desdemona' has orange flowers that make a bold statement, appearing on erect stems well above the foliage. Other striking ligularias are available, including the stately 'The Rocket', which can hit 6ft (2m) high. Take precautions against slugs and snails, which can be a major nuisance.

OTHER VARIETIES *L. dentata* 'Othello' (deep purplish green leaves); *L.* 'Gregynog Gold' (taller-growing, golden-orange flowers); *L.* 'The Rocket' (taller-growing, yellow flowers on black stems).

PLANT PROFILE
HEIGHT 3ft (1m)
SPREAD 24in (60cm)
SITE Partial shade
SOIL Moist, fertile
HARDINESS Z4–8 H8–1
FLOWERING Midsummer to early autumn

L

Ligularia przewalskii Golden ray

STRIKING, TALL, AND SHOWY, this plant combines three good colors in midsummer: dark green leaves, thin black flower stems, and tall columns of bright yellow tiny flowers. *Ligularia przewalskii* is very effective when planted *en masse* or in small groups dotted through a border, making the eye zigzag from one group of yellow spires to another. There is not much difference between this and 'The Rocket', although the leaves of *L. przewalskii* are more dramatically jagged. Moist soil that doesn't dry out in summer is essential—without this, ligularias need copious watering.

OTHER VARIETIES *L. dentata* (smaller-growing, clusters of orange-yellow flowers); *L. hodgsonii* (smaller-growing, yellow-orange flowers).

PLANT PROFILE

HEIGHT To 6ft (2m)

SPREAD 3ft (1m)

SITE Full sun

SOIL Moist, fertile

HARDINESS Z5–8 H8–1

FLOWERING Mid- and late summer

Limonium latifolium Sea lavender

L

THE FOAMING MASS OF LAVENDER-BLUE flowers liberally covering the foliage of this plant is an impressive sight. Sea lavender is small enough for most sites and, with its tolerance of salt spray, is typically seen in coastal gardens, where it benefits from free-draining soil and bright sun. The flowers of most types of sea lavender are used in displays of cut flowers and for drying. The main problem that affects this plant is powdery mildew, a fungal disease that causes a white, powdery growth on the leaves. It can be kept in check by ensuring that the soil is not too dry, or by using commercial sprays.

OTHER VARIETIES *L. bellidifolium* (smaller-growing, pale violet or blue-violet flowers); *L. platyphyllum* 'Violetta' (deep violet flowers).

PLANT PROFILE
HEIGHT 24in (60cm) or more
SPREAD 18in (45cm)
SITE Full sun
SOIL Free-draining
HARDINESS Z4–9 H9–1
FLOWERING Late summer

L

Linaria purpurea 'Canon Went' Toadflax

WITH CLUSTERS OF PALE PINK FLOWERS at the top of tall, thin stems, 'Canon Went' is ideal for cottage gardens, where it adds a free-flowing, open look. Although short-lived, it self-seeds freely and you never have to worry about raising replacements, although if you want to retain the pink color, you must keep it away from *Linaria purpurea*, with which it will crossbreed. To keep it in check, remove any unwanted new plants in the spring, and transplant others to a more desirable site. Full sun and good drainage are required.

OTHER VARIETIES *L. dalmatica* (yellow flowers); *L. purpurea* (violet-purple flowers); *L. purpurea* 'Springside White' (white flowers); *L. triornithophora* (purple and yellow flowers with brownish purple spurs).

PLANT PROFILE
HEIGHT 3ft (1m)
SPREAD 12in (30cm)
SITE Full sun
SOIL Free-draining
HARDINESS Z5–8 H8–5
FLOWERING Early summer to early autumn

Linum perenne Perennial flax

L

WITH A CONSTANT SUCCESSION of flowers giving a show of bright blue throughout summer, you don't notice that each flower lasts only a single day. A sunny situation is essential because the blooms tend to stay firmly closed when it's dull and cloudy. A low-growing plant, perennial flax should be placed at the front of a border and planted in light, free-draining soil. The flax is at its best for the first few years, and you should replace it either with cuttings after three years or with one of its seedlings. *Linum narbonense* (flowering flax) is a good alternative—it is slightly bluer, and often lives longer.

OTHER VARIETIES *L. flavum* (smaller-growing, gold flowers); *L.* 'Gemmell's Hybrid' (smaller-growing, chrome yellow flowers).

PLANT PROFILE	
HEIGHT 4–24in (10–60cm)	
SPREAD 12in (30cm)	
SITE Partial shade	
SOIL Free-draining	
HARDINESS Z5–8 H8–5	
FLOWERING Early and midsummer	

L   *Liriope muscari* Lilyturf

IN CHINA AND JAPAN, lilyturf grows naturally in the acidic soil of the woodland floor, and these are the garden conditions it needs—moist but free-draining soil and shelter. The autumn show, with scores of tiny violet-mauve flowers packed around an upright stem, is made even better by the evergreen, strap-shaped leaves. It can be invasive, but if clumps spread too far, slice off the roots with a spade and dig out excess growth. Other good liriopes include 'Monroe White' and 'Variegata', which has creamy white striped leaves.

OTHER VARIETIES   *L. muscari* 'John Burch' (gold-variegated leaves); *L. muscari* 'Monroe White' (white flowers, needs full shade); *L. spicata* (smaller-growing, violet to white flowers).

PLANT PROFILE
HEIGHT 12in (30cm)
SPREAD 18in (45cm)
SITE Partial or full shade
SOIL Moist but free-draining
HARDINESS Z6–10 H10–6
FLOWERING Early to late autumn

Lobelia cardinalis Cardinal flower

L

VIVID SCARLET FLOWERS above dark bronze leaves make this lobelia an essential ingredient for a hot color scheme. It needs moist soil, however, so if there is any danger of its drying out, add a thick mulch of compost after watering. It is well worth growing a large clump of these plants, partly to make sure lots survive the attention of slugs, and partly because the scarlet flowers makes a striking display. It can also be grown in bog gardens and in shallow water.

OTHER VARIETIES *L. dortmanna* (smaller-growing, blue to pale violet flowers, grows in shallow water); *L.* x *gerardii* 'Vedrariensis' (larger-growing, violet-purple flowers); *L. laxiflora* (yellow flowers, red-tinted stems); *L.* 'Queen Victoria' (scarlet flowers).

PLANT PROFILE

HEIGHT 3ft (1m)

SPREAD 12in (30cm)

SITE Full sun or partial shade

SOIL Moist

HARDINESS Z2–8 H8–1

FLOWERING Summer and early autumn

L

Lunaria rediviva Perennial honesty

GROWING NATURALLY ON THE EDGES of woodlands, this plant is just right for cottage gardens or for the wilder, outer fringes of a more formal garden design. It has dark green leaves, about 5in (13cm) long or more, with small, delicate, pale lilac-white flowers. The flowers also have a gentle scent. Provide moist, fertile soil for the best results. Like the annual *Lunaria annua*, it produces excellent seedheads that look like silver coins, which is why perennial honesty is sometimes called the money plant. The seedheads can be dried and used in decorative displays.

PLANT PROFILE

HEIGHT 24–36in (60–90cm)

SPREAD 12in (30cm)

SITE Full sun or partial shade

SOIL Moist, fertile

HARDINESS Z6–9 H9–6

FLOWERING Late spring and early summer

Lupinus 'My Castle' Lupin

L

ALTHOUGH LUPINS ENCOMPASS annuals and shrubs, this is a clump-forming, soft-red perennial. It mixes well with other lively-colored lupins, and there are plenty available, such as 'Chandelier' (bright yellow), 'The Chatelaine' (pink and white) and 'The Governor' (blue and white). All prefer free-draining soil that is not too rich. Grow new plants from seed, or take cuttings as soon as the new growth starts. Because lupins are prone to various diseases and are short-lived, you will need to replace them every few years.

OTHER VARIETIES *L.* Band of Nobles Series (white, yellow, pink, red, blue, or bicolored); *L.* 'Noble Maiden' (creamy white flowers); *L.* 'Thundercloud' (deep violet-blue flowers).

PLANT PROFILE
HEIGHT 3ft (1m)
SPREAD 30in (75cm)
SITE Full sun or partial shade
SOIL Fertile, free-draining
HARDINESS Z4–7 H7–1
FLOWERING Early and midsummer

L | *Luzula nivea* Snowy woodrush

THE MOST POPULAR TYPES of woodrush are *Luzula nivea* and the many varieties of *L. sylvatica* (greater woodrush). They are evergreen wild garden or woodland plants that require moist, rich soil and shade. You can grow them out in the open if the soil is mulched with compost and remains damp. *L. nivea* has bright white flowers above grasslike leaves, while the flowers of *L. sylvatica* make an earlier display, opening in midspring. *L. sylvatica* 'Aurea' is an attractive winter performer because of its bright yellow leaves.

OTHER VARIETIES *L. sylvatica* (chestnut brown flowers); *L. sylvatica* 'Marginata' (pendent, brown and gold flowers, rich green leaves with neat cream margins).

PLANT PROFILE

HEIGHT 24in (60cm)

SPREAD 18in (45cm)

SITE Partial or deep shade

SOIL Moist, fertile

HARDINESS Z4–9 H9–1

FLOWERING Early and midsummer

Lychnis chalcedonica Jerusalem cross

THE BRIGHT SCARLET FLOWERS of Jerusalem cross immediately grab your attention, and they can be used effectively as a background plant to *Verbena bonariensis*, in knot gardens, and in flashy hot-color plans. It self-seeds freely and clumps soon form, but they need some support to prevent their heads from flopping and ruining the colorful impact. They don't flower beyond midsummer and should be planted next to flowering plants that will keep the show going. The soil needs to be moist, rich, and free-draining.

OTHER VARIETIES *L. coronaria* (shorter, purple-red flowers, silver-gray leaves); *L. coronaria* 'Alba' (white flowers); *L. coronata* var. *sieboldii* (deep red flowers); *L. flos-cuculi* (shorter, bright purplish pink).

PLANT PROFILE
HEIGHT 3–4ft (1–1.2m)
SPREAD 12in (30cm)
SITE Full sun or partial shade
SOIL Fertile, moist but free-draining
HARDINESS Z4–8 H8–1
FLOWERING Early and midsummer

L | *Lychnis coronaria* Rose campion

THIS COTTAGE-GARDEN FAVORITE features strong color contrasts, making it popular in borders as well. The soft leaves are silver-gray, while the flowers are like flat, purple-red disks. Free-draining soil and constant sun are the keys to success here, and the stems will need staking in exposed, windy gardens to prevent them from flopping. The downy foliage of young plants may be visible throughout a mild winter. Although short-lived, it self-seeds, giving rise to more plants that you can easily fork out and replant to fill any gaps.

OTHER VARIETIES *L.* x *arkwrightii* 'Vesuvius' (smaller-growing, orange-scarlet flowers, brownish green leaves); *L. chalcedonica* (taller-growing, scarlet flowers).

PLANT PROFILE
HEIGHT 32in (80cm)
SPREAD 18in (45cm)
SITE Full sun
SOIL Free-draining
HARDINESS Z4–8 H8–1
FLOWERING Late summer

Lysichiton americanus Yellow skunk cabbage

L

GROWING IN THE MUDDY, shallow water of large ponds or streams, the curious flowers of the yellow skunk cabbage produce a flashy touch of bright color. The flowers are actually attached to the central pokerlike growth, and what looks like a giant petal is, in fact, a spathe, or colored bract (in Greek, *Lysichiton* means a loose cloak). Both appear before the large, glossy, veined leaves, which, with luck, can grow as long as 4ft (1.2m), so make sure you provide enough space for them to develop.

OTHER VARIETY *L. camtschatcensis* (green poker and contrasting white spathe, strongly veined dark green leaves).

PLANT PROFILE

HEIGHT 3ft (1m)

SPREAD 4ft (1.2m)

SITE Full sun or partial shade

SOIL Moist

HARDINESS Z7–9 H9–7

FLOWERING Early spring

L

Lysimachia clethroides Loosestrife

ALTHOUGH IT CAN BE INVASIVE, *Lysimachia clethroides* looks best when grown in showy groups. The spires, initially with a crook at the top, have tiny white flowers running up to the tip. Loosestrife needs moist soil and is usually grown either in light shade with a heavy mulch of compost or near natural ponds. A good alternative is the slightly tender, white-flowering *L. epherum*, which tends to bloom more in the first half of summer. Any excess growth can be controlled by digging out unwanted plants.

OTHER VARIETIES *L. ciliata* (taller-growing, yellow flowers with reddish centers); *L. nummularia* 'Aurea' (smaller-growing groundcover, yellow flowers and leaves).

PLANT PROFILE

HEIGHT 3ft (1m)

SPREAD 24in (60cm)

SITE Full sun or partial shade

SOIL Moist

HARDINESS Z4–9 H9–1

FLOWERING Mid- and late summer

Lysimachia punctata Loosestrife

L

THIS QUIRKY PLANT sends up stiff, vertical flower stems with short, horizontal leaves ranged up the spire between bright yellow flowers. It is quite invasive, and will soon form a showy colony in the damp soil near a natural pond. You can also grow it in a moist border, although it may intrude on its neighbors, in which case you will have to slice the roots with a spade and dig out any excess growth. A much smaller alternative is the 2in- (5cm-) high, yellow-leaved *Lysimachia nummularia* 'Aurea', which is also invasive but makes good groundcover.

OTHER VARIETIES *L. clethroides* (white flowers, mid-green leaves); *L. vulgaris* (larger-growing, yellow flowers, bright green leaves).

PLANT PROFILE
HEIGHT 3ft (1m)
SPREAD 24in (60cm)
SITE Full sun or partial shade
SOIL Moist
HARDINESS Z4–8 H8–1
FLOWERING Mid- and late summer

L

Lythrum salicaria Purple loosestrife

NOT TO BE CONFUSED with *Lysimachia*, which is also known as loosestrife and thrives in moist soil, this plant has thin spires covered with rose red flowers. Though undeniably attractive, the nonnative *Lythrum salicaria* is notorious for escaping into the wild and harming fragile wetland ecosystems by crowding out native plants, and it is not recommended for most garden situations. For an eco-friendly, native alternative, try planting *Liatris spicata* (p.185).

PLANT PROFILE
HEIGHT 3ft (1m)
SPREAD 18in (45cm)
SITE Full sun
SOIL Moist
HARDINESS Z4–9 H9–1
FLOWERING Midsummer to early autumn

Macleaya cordata Plume poppy

M

WITH ITS GRAY-GREEN STEMS and masses of airy, plumelike flowers, this is an excellent choice for a large border. It needs small plants in front so that its large, shapely, gray to olive green leaves are not obscured. Plume poppies like rich moist but free-draining soil, although they will tolerate less-than-ideal conditions and even some shade. Remove excess spreading growth to keep the plant in check. An alternative choice is *Macleaya microcarpa* 'Kelway's Coral Plume' which has coral-pink flowers and is slightly more invasive.

OTHER VARIETIES *M. cordata* 'Flamingo' (buff-pink flowers from pink buds); *M.* x *kewensis* (creamy buff flowers, gray-green leaves).

PLANT PROFILE
HEIGHT To 8ft (2.5m)
SPREAD 3ft (1m)
SITE Full sun
SOIL Fertile, moist but free-draining
HARDINESS Z4–8 H8–1
FLOWERING Mid- and late summer

M | *Maianthemum bifolium* False lily-of-the-valley

PROVIDING GOOD GROUNDCOVER, false lily-of-the-valley produces a low, quick-spreading mat of glossy leaves. Out of each clump of leaves, stems carrying four-petaled flowers appear in the spring (in mild weather) or early summer, and these are followed by small, bright red berries. Due to its invasive nature, this is definitely not a plant for the border; instead, grow it in wild or woodland gardens where it can multiply freely. The soil should be rich and moist, without being boggy, and neutral to slightly acidic.

PLANT PROFILE

HEIGHT 6in (15cm)

SPREAD Indefinite

SITE Light dappled or deep shade

SOIL Fertile, moist but free-draining

HARDINESS Z4–5 H5–1

FLOWERING Early summer

Malva moschata f. *alba* Musk mallow

AVAILABLE IN SHADES OF WHITE, PINK, blue, and purple, mallows are frustratingly short-lived, although they do self-seed. This form of the plant has gently scented white flowers that gradually take on a pink tinge, and is a good candidate for a cottage garden. It is bushy and stands up straight, and can be planted alongside the pink-flowered *Malva moschata*. Both need free-draining soil and some support when grown on exposed, windy sites. If they are being grown on heavy clay soil, treat them as annuals—collect seed in the autumn and grow new plants each year.

OTHER VARIETIES *M. alcea* var. *fastigiata* (smaller-growing, deep pink flowers); *M. sylvestris* (veined pinkish purple flowers).

PLANT PROFILE
HEIGHT 3ft (1m)
SPREAD 24in (60cm)
SITE Full sun
SOIL Free-draining
HARDINESS Z4–8 H8–1
FLOWERING Early summer to early autumn

M | *Meconopsis betonicifolia* Himalayan blue poppy

THE TIBETAN BLUE POPPY, as it is also known, is an absolute delight. It has open, clear blue flowers with four petals and an inner eye of yellow anthers. It needs a cool climate and soil that never dries out, remaining moist all summer. If you have suitable conditions for this poppy, plant it in drifts or small groups in a border. If conditions are less than favorable, it will flower in its first summer and then die, but even as an annual it's definitely worth growing. You can raise it from seed, but it's easier to buy new young plants.

OTHER VARIETIES   *M. grandis* (rich blue to purplish red flowers); *M. napaulensis* (larger-growing, pink, red, or purple flowers).

PLANT PROFILE
HEIGHT 4ft (1.2m)
SPREAD 18in (45cm)
SITE Partial shade
SOIL Moist
HARDINESS Z7–8 H8–7
FLOWERING Early summer

Meconopsis cambrica Welsh poppy

M

GROWING WILD IN WALES in shady areas where the soil is moist, the Welsh poppy will, with luck, self-seed around the garden. If you find seedlings popping up in open, hot, dry areas, move them immediately so that their roots are in moist, cool soil. Welsh poppies flower throughout the summer months, and even a single plant, if it is strategically placed, can be a real gem. Use it in a shady spot in a wildflower garden or to brighten up a bed beneath trees or shrubs.

OTHER VARIETIES *M. quintuplinervia* (pale lavender-blue or purplish blue flowers); *M.* x *sheldonii* (larger-growing, deep rich to pale blue flowers).

PLANT PROFILE

HEIGHT 18in (45cm)

SPREAD 10in (25cm)

SITE Partial shade

SOIL Moist

HARDINESS Z6–8 H8–6

FLOWERING Midspring to midautumn

M | *Melianthus major* Honey bush

A MUST FOR GARDENS featuring architectural plants, *Melianthus major* has beautiful, shapely leaves, each up to 20in (50cm) long. Technically a shrub, it performs like a perennial in cold-climate gardens because the topgrowth dies back in winter; even if it does not die, it should be pruned to the ground in spring. Later, superb, fresh, multifingered leaves open before the insignificant flowers appear. Plants need a sheltered, sunny position on moist but free-draining, fertile ground. Provide a thick winter mulch of compost to protect the young roots and, although mature plants should survive bad winters, keep on mulching. It makes a good combination when positioned behind eryngiums (sea holly)—both have shapely foliage, with that of the latter being smaller and spiky.

PLANT PROFILE

HEIGHT 6–10ft (2–3m)

SPREAD 3–10ft (1–3m)

SITE Full sun

SOIL Fertile, moist but free-draining

HARDINESS Z8–11 H12–8

FLOWERING Late spring to midsummer

Melica altissima 'Atropurpurea' Siberian melick

M

NATIVE TO CENTRAL AND EASTERN EUROPE, this decorative grass grows in shrubby thickets and at the edges of forests. It makes an upright clump with purple-mauve flower spikes that gradually fade in color as they age. 'Atropurpurea' grows equally well in light shade or hot, sunny sites, and the foliage can be left to stand over winter, adding shape and interest to the garden—cut it away in spring before the new growth begins. 'Alba' has white flower spikes, and both forms are useful in cut-flower displays.

OTHER VARIETIES *M. nutans* (smaller-growing, brown and cream flower spikes from late-spring, fresh green leaves); *M. uniflora* 'Variegata' (smaller-growing, fresh green leaves with creamy stripes).

PLANT PROFILE	
HEIGHT To 5ft (1.5m)	
SPREAD To 32in (80cm)	
SITE Full sun or light shade	
SOIL Moist, free-draining	
HARDINESS Z5–8 H8–5	
FLOWERING Summer	

M | *Melissa officinalis* 'Aurea' Lemon balm

For Mediterranean-style or herb gardens, pots, or borders, this plant is perfect. It is widely grown for its lemon-scented, yellow-splashed leaves, although the color tends to fade in summer. The flowers are pale and small, and should be cut off once they start to fade to prevent self-seeding. Lemon balm needs light, free-draining soil that is quite poor; if it sits in cold, wet soil it will rot. When using the leaves for potpourri or cooking, keep in mind that they are at their most highly scented as the flowers start to open in early summer.

OTHER VARIETIES *M. officinalis* (pale yellow flowers, light green leaves); *M. officinalis* 'All Gold' (white flowers, yellow leaves).

PLANT PROFILE
HEIGHT 24–48in (60–120cm)
SPREAD 12–18in (30–45cm)
SITE Full sun
SOIL Poor, free-draining
HARDINESS Z3–7 H7–1
FLOWERING Summer

Melittis melissophyllum Bastard balm

M

IN THE WILD, this plant grows in patchy woodland in Europe. It is related to deadnettles and has unusual, spotted flowers, about 1½in (4cm) long, with pink or purple lips. The flowers appear in clusters of two to six, and act as a magnet for bees, while the leaves have the gentle scent of honey. If you cannot reproduce a woodland-type setting in your garden, then use *Melittis melissophyllum* at the front of a border, but you must provide partial shade and moist, free-draining soil that never becomes too dry. Propagate plants by division in the spring, just as the new growth gets under way.

PLANT PROFILE

HEIGHT 8–28in (20–70cm)

SPREAD 20in (50cm)

SITE Partial shade

SOIL Moist, free-draining

HARDINESS Z6–9 H9–6

FLOWERING Late spring and early summer

M *Mentha suaveolens* 'Variegata' Pineapple mint

THIS IS A STRIKING VARIEGATED plant, with soft hairy leaves with the scent of pineapple. The eye-catching foliage and the fact that it is not rampantly invasive make it a good choice for herb gardens. Like most mints, its spread can be controlled by planting it in a sunken, bottomless bucket filled with moist, infertile soil. Sections can be snipped off and planted in large pots to bring indoors over winter, when the leaves can be used to flavor peas, beans, lamb, and fish, as well as homemade lemonade.

OTHER VARIETIES *M. aquatica* (smaller-growing maginal aquatic, lilac flowers, aromatic dark green leaves); *M. longifolia* (taller-growing, lilac or white flowers, musty-scented silver-gray leaves).

PLANT PROFILE	
HEIGHT To 3ft (1m)	
SPREAD Indefinite	
SITE Full sun	
SOIL Moist	
HARDINESS Z6–9 H9–5	
FLOWERING Summer	

Milium effusum 'Aureum' Bowles' golden grass

M

IN THE SPRING when the young, strap-shaped foliage is a bright, vivid, yellowish green, this perennial looks extremely striking. It makes an even better show in light shade—its preferred site— adding much-needed color to these areas. By midsummer the leaves have lost much of their fresh color and turn slightly green. 'Aureum' rarely lives for long, but it is a modest self-seeder and should provide a steady supply of replacements. The soil needs to be moist and rich. If 'Aureum' is being grown in a more open, sunnier position, apply a thick mulch of compost to lock moisture in the ground.

OTHER VARIETY *M. effusum* 'Yaffle' (taller-growing, golden leaves with a pale green stripe).

PLANT PROFILE	
HEIGHT To 24in (60cm)	
SPREAD 12in (30cm)	
SITE Partial shade	
SOIL Moist, fertile	
HARDINESS Z6–9 H9–6	
FLOWERING Late spring to midsummer	

Fully fluffed-up grass heads, or inflorescences (above), are full of seeds. If you cut the stems too soon (top), the head will contain unripe seed.

M *Miscanthus sinensis* 'Silberfeder' Eulalia grass

SOME OF THE BEST flowering grasses available for gardens are found in this group of plants, and at 8ft (2.5m), 'Silberfeder' is one of the tallest. The large clump of foliage is topped by beautiful plumes of feathery flowerheads, held up high to catch the breeze. The thin, straplike leaves are on the lax side, and tend to arch over and flop, which gives 'Silberfeder' a rather graceful look. The grasses grow in most gardens, enjoying decent drainage and average fertility.

OTHER VARIETIES *M. sinensis* 'Rotsilber' (smaller-growing, red-tinted silver heads); *M. sinensis* 'Zebrinus' (smaller-growing, arching leaves with creamy white or pale yellow horizontal bands).

PLANT PROFILE	
HEIGHT 8ft (2.5m)	
SPREAD 4ft (1.2m)	
SITE Full sun	
SOIL Average, free-draining	
HARDINESS Z4–9 H9–1	
FLOWERING Autumn	

Molinia caerulea subsp. *caerulea* 'Moorhexe' Purple moor grass

M

MOST OF THE MOLINIAS are tall grasses, up to 7ft (2.2m) high, but this is an extremely useful small moor grass. Smartly upright with green leaves, it needs a position right at the front of a border, or you could plant it in groups around the feet of a pergola. For a much bigger plant, go for a form of *Molinia caerulea* subsp. *arundinacea*, such as the tall, very upright 'Sky Racer'. All moor grasses have rich, yellow-orange tints in the autumn, and should be grown in moist but free-draining, acidic to neutral soil.

OTHER VARIETIES *M. caerulea* subsp. *arundinacea* 'Karl Foerster' (larger-growing, purple flowerheads on arching stems); *M. caerulea* subsp. *caerulea* 'Variegata' (cream-striped leaves, ocher stems).

PLANT PROFILE	
HEIGHT 18in (45cm)	
SPREAD 16in (40cm)	
SITE Full sun or partial shade	
SOIL Moist but free-draining	
HARDINESS Z5–9	
FLOWERING Spring to autumn	

M | *Moltkia doerfleri*

WITH ITS SPECIFIC CULTIVATION REQUIREMENTS, which include very free-draining soil with average to poor fertility, *Moltkia doerfleri* is a perfect plant for the top of a stone wall, or a rock or gravel garden. Its stiff, wiry, erect stems are covered in deep purple flowers in the first part of summer, often starting in late spring, and the leaves are mid-green, narrowly lance-shaped, and about 2in (5cm) long. Although hardy, it dislikes being exposed to icy winds and standing in wet soil, preferring a sheltered, warm position. Other types tend to be shrubby with blue, purple, or yellow flowers.

PLANT PROFILE

HEIGHT 12–20in (30–50cm)

SPREAD 12–20in (30–50cm)

SITE Full sun

SOIL Poor, free-draining

HARDINESS Z7–9

FLOWERING Late spring to midsummer

Monarda 'Cambridge Scarlet' **Bergamot**

M

THE MIDSUMMER FLOWERS of this plant are a combination of rich red and scarlet and look best when grown in groups in a border. They make a striking show, but are likely to upstage any nearby pastel colors. Many monardas have leaves with a strong citrus scent suitable for potpourri. Moist, rich soil is the key to success in summer, but you must avoid wet ground in winter. Mulch plants well to lock in soil moisture and to help prevent powdery mildew, which can be a major problem during long hot spells.

OTHER VARIETIES *M.* 'Beauty of Cobham' (pink flowers, purple bracts); *M.* 'Croftway Pink' (rose pink flowers and bracts); *M. didyma* (pink flowers, red bracts); *M.* 'Vintage Wine' (reddish flowers, brown bracts).

PLANT PROFILE	
HEIGHT 3ft (1m)	
SPREAD 18in (45cm)	
SITE Full sun or dappled shade	
SOIL Fertile, moist but free-draining	
HARDINESS Z4–9 H9–1	
FLOWERING Midsummer to early autumn	

M | *Morina longifolia* Whorlflower

A ROSETTE OF SHINY, spiny evergreen leaves, each up to 12in (30cm) long, appears on the ground, giving this plant an intriguing, striking look. From the rosette a vertical flowering stem shoots up. The white flowers grow in whorls or tiers up the stem, and the blooms are held in green bracts. It is fussy in its requirements, and to ensure success in colder zones, the crown needs a winter covering of mulch to protect it from wind and frost, while the roots demand free-draining soil that never bakes dry. Before planting, dig well-rotted compost into the soil to improve its structure.

PLANT PROFILE

HEIGHT 3ft (1m) or more

SPREAD 20in (50cm)

SITE Full sun

SOIL Free-draining

HARDINESS Z6–9 H9–6

FLOWERING Midsummer

Nemesia denticulata

N

IN ITS NATIVE SOUTHERN AFRICA, this plant grows in sandy, rocky sites, and produces flowers mainly in pink, mauve, and white. In the garden, the small, scented flowers need to be placed at the front of a display or they can be overlooked. In colder regions, grow it in a warm, sheltered position with very good drainage—at the base of a sunny wall, for example—or pot it in the autumn and keep it in a frost-free greenhouse until the following spring. If growing it outdoors, cut the stems back in spring once frosts are over, and water well during dry spells.

OTHER VARIETIES *N. caerulea* (taller-growing, pink, pale blue, lavender-blue, or white flowers); *N.* 'Innocence' (white flowers).

PLANT PROFILE
HEIGHT 10in (25cm)
SPREAD 12in (30cm)
SITE Full sun
SOIL Moist, free-draining
HARDINESS Z8–9
FLOWERING Summer to early autumn

N | *Nepeta sibirica* Catmint

IF YOU WANT TO DRIVE CATS WILD and attract bees to your garden, this is the plant for you. It has strongly scented, dark gray leaves and a haze of light blue flowers. Shorter catmints, such as *Nepeta racemosa*, are best planted at the front of a border or edging a path, but this tall variety can be placed further back. The soil should be free-draining and on the dry side, although some types, such as *N. subsessilis*, are suitable for shady, moist gardens.

OTHER VARIETIES *N. govaniana* (yellow flowers, shady, moist sites); *N. sibirica* 'Souvenir d'André Chaudron' (smaller-growing, dark lavender-blue flowers, gray-green leaves); *N.* 'Six Hills Giant' (lavender-blue flowers, gray-green leaves); *N. subsessilis* (bright blue flowers, shady, moist sites).

PLANT PROFILE
HEIGHT 3ft (1m)
SPREAD 18in (45cm)
SITE Full sun or partial shade
SOIL Free-draining
HARDINESS Z3–8 H8–1
FLOWERING Mid- and late summer

Nicotiana sylvestris Tobacco plant

TALL, UPRIGHT, AND SCENTED, this tall tobacco plant makes a classy ingredient for a cottage garden, as well as for more formal designs. The stems shoot up from large, ground-hugging leaves, which can reach a length of 14in (35cm), and hold long, thin, tubular, white flowers with a rich, sweet scent. Plant *Nicotiana sylvestris* in clumps, or circles around a feature plant, in rich, free-draining soil. It is short-lived, but is easy to grow from seed collected in the autumn. Leave space for the large leaves or they will obscure smaller, neighboring plants as they grow.

OTHER VARIETIES *N. alata* (greenish yellow flowers, white within); *N. x sanderae* (red, rose pink, purple, or sometimes white flowers).

PLANT PROFILE
HEIGHT To 5ft (1.5m)
SPREAD To 24in (60cm)
SITE Full sun or partial shade
SOIL Fertile, free-draining
HARDINESS Z10–11 H12–1
FLOWERING Summer

O *Oenanthe javanica* 'Flamingo' Water celery

GROWING IN BOG GARDENS or water meadows, or close to natural ponds or streams, the moisture-loving 'Flamingo' produces attractive pink, cream, and white foliage. The tiny, star-shaped white flowers appear in small sprays in the second half of summer and, with the clusters of multicolored leaves on long stalks, make useful components in cut-flower displays. Don't be put off by some reports that 'Flamingo' is highly toxic—it is safe, and is even eaten as a vegetable in some regions of the world (from India to Japan). Other types of *Oenanthe*, however, are toxic.

PLANT PROFILE

HEIGHT 8–16in (20–40cm)

SPREAD 3ft (1m)

SITE Full sun or partial shade

SOIL Moist

HARDINESS Z9–11 H12–9

FLOWERING Late summer

Oenothera fruticosa 'Fyrverkeri' Evening primrose

O

JAZZING UP THE SUMMER GARDEN, the flowers of this plant are startlingly bright yellow, shaped like saucers, and arranged all the way up short, red-tinged stems. 'Fyrverkeri', which is also known as 'Fireworks', scores even more points because its young leaves have a reddish purple tinge, making a lively contrast with the stems. It needs to be positioned with care, and kept away from plants with more subdued colors, since these will be pushed into the background once the flowers open. The key to success with evening primrose is sandy, free-draining soil.

OTHER VARIETIES *O. fruticosa* subsp. *glauca* (light yellow flowers); *O. fruticosa* subsp. *glauca* 'Erica Robin' (young red foliage, golden flowers).

PLANT PROFILE

HEIGHT 12–40in (30–100cm)

SPREAD 12in (30cm)

SITE Full sun

SOIL Free-draining

HARDINESS Z4–8 H8–1

FLOWERING Late spring to late summer

O | *Omphalodes cappadocica* 'Cherry Ingram' Navelwort

THE LARGE, DARK BLUE FLOWERS with white centers make 'Cherry Ingram' a better choice than the parent plant, *Omphalodes cappadocica*, which has smaller, lighter flowers. This is a pretty plant for a wild garden or for growing among shrubs in the border, adding sprays of blue in the early spring. It is particularly valuable because it tolerates a shady garden position, and where grown on moist, rich soil will make attractive clumps. Navelwort mixes well with primulas that like the same site and soil conditions. A good alternative is 'Starry Eyes', which has a white stripe on each petal.

OTHER VARIETIES *O. cappadocica* 'Lilac Mist' (lilac-blue flowers); *O. verna* (blue, smaller flowers).

PLANT PROFILE

HEIGHT To 10in (25cm)

SPREAD To 16in (40cm)

SITE Partial shade

SOIL Moist, fertile

HARDINESS Z6–8 H8–6

FLOWERING Early spring

Ophiopogon planiscapus 'Nigrescens' Lilyturf

O

APPEARANCES CAN BE DECEPTIVE. Although this plant looks like a miniature, black-leaved grass with outward-radiating, splayed leaves, it is, in fact, an evergreen perennial. 'Nigrescens' is often used to set off larger, more dominant architectural plants, such as cordylines or yuccas. The black leaves stand out well against pale gravel, and it requires slightly acidic, free-draining, fertile soil. *Ophiopogon jaburan* 'Vittatus' is another worthwhile, though less hardy, lilyturf with green- and cream-striped leaves.

OTHER VARIETIES *O. japonicus* (taller-growing, white, bell-shaped flowers, dark green leaves, blue-black berries); *O. planiscapus* (pale purplish white flowers, dark green leaves, blue-black berries)

PLANT PROFILE
HEIGHT 8in (20cm)
SPREAD 12in (30cm)
SITE Full sun or light shade
SOIL Acidic, fertile, free-draining
HARDINESS Z6–11 H12–1
FLOWERING Summer

O   *Osteospermum jucundum* African daisy

LARGE, BRIGHT, DAISYLIKE FLOWERS are the chief characteristic of osteospermums, some, such as 'Whirligig', with petals like outward-radiating spokes with a tiny bulge at the end. They need plenty of sun and free-draining soil, and most won't survive cold, wet winters. This is one of the hardiest, however, and throughout the summer it produces mauve-pink flowers with a yellow eye. It makes a good-size clump for the front of a border or softening the edges of a path.

OTHER VARIETIES *O.* 'Buttermilk' (larger-growing, primrose yellow flowers with a bluish mauve eye); *O.* 'Cannington Roy' (smaller-growing, purple-tipped white flowers with a purple eye); *O. ecklonis* (larger-growing, white flowers, indigo blue on the reverse, with a dark blue eye).

PLANT PROFILE
HEIGHT 10in (25cm)
SPREAD 20–36in (50–90cm)
SITE Full sun
SOIL Free-draining
HARDINESS Z9–11 H6–1
FLOWERING Late spring to autumn

Oxalis 'Ione Hecker' Shamrock

THE DIMINUTIVE SIZE of this perennial demands a place in a rock garden, raised bed, or trough. The flowers have five petals with thin, dark purple veins, and it has small, ornamental leaves. Other equally pretty types are available, such as the purple-pink *Oxalis adenophylla*, the yellow *O. lobata*, and *O. versicolor*, which has white flowers with crimson margins on the underside. These oxalis like free-draining soil, and although 'Ione Hecker' is fairly hardy, the others need a sunny, sheltered position to survive in cold-climate gardens.

OTHER VARIETIES *O. depressa* (rose pink to purple-pink flowers); *O. enneaphylla* 'Minutifolia' (compact with white flowers); *O. laciniata* (fragrant, lilac-blue, red, pink, or white flowers).

PLANT PROFILE	
HEIGHT 3in (8cm)	
SPREAD 4in (10cm)	
SITE Full or partial shade	
SOIL Free-draining	
HARDINESS Z8–9 H9–8	
FLOWERING Summer	

P

Pachyphragma macrophyllum

FOR LIGHT SHADE AND MOIST, leafy soil, this plant is a real garden asset. It flowers before the leaves have fully developed and provides sprays of fresh, white petals. Although not exactly invasive, it does provide good cover underneath trees and deciduous shrubs, where it creeps and spreads across the soil. After the vivid show of flowers is finished, semievergreen, glossy, dark green leaves fill out and help to suppress any emerging weeds. It may be tempting to cut the flowers for use in an indoor display, but it is worth noting that they do have a slightly unpleasant smell.

PLANT PROFILE

HEIGHT 8–16in (20–40cm)

SPREAD 24–36in (60–90cm)

SITE Partial shade

SOIL Moist

HARDINESS Z5–9 H9–5

FLOWERING Early spring

Pachysandra terminalis Japanese spurge

P

THIS EVERGREEN PLANT IS SUITABLE for even the densest shade in the garden. Its stems spread vigorously, rooting as they go, to make carpets of shiny green foliage. The leaves grow almost in rosettes and are about 4in (10cm) long, pointing outward. Short flower spikes appear in the spring, with tiny white flowers opening at the end of the season or in early summer. *Pachysandra terminalis* needs moist soil with plenty of leaf mold incorporated into it; this plant will not succeed in dry shade. A good, slightly less vigorous alternative is *P. terminalis* 'Variegata' which has attractive creamy white markings on the edges of its leaves.

OTHER VARIETY *P. terminalis* 'Green Carpet' (finely toothed leaves).

PLANT PROFILE

HEIGHT 8in (20cm)

SPREAD Indefinite

SITE Full or partial shade

SOIL Moist

HARDINESS Z4–8 H8–1

FLOWERING Late spring

P

Paeonia lactiflora 'Sarah Bernhardt' Peony

THE SUMPTUOUS FLOWERS of peonies provide some of the best garden displays. There is a wide choice of colors, mainly white, yellow, red, and pink, and the flowers often have a spicy scent. 'Sarah Bernhardt' is scented, soft pink with frilly petals. If space allows, also grow the pink 'Bowl of Beauty', white 'Félix Crousse', and yellow *Paeonia mlokosewitschii*. All should be more to the front than the middle of a border so that they can be fully appreciated. Provide rich, moist but free-draining soil, and support for the stems. Once in the ground and established, they don't like to be disturbed.

OTHER VARIETIES *P. cambessedesii* (smaller-growing, single, deep pink flowers); *P. lactiflora* (single, fragrant, white to pale pink flowers).

PLANT PROFILE
HEIGHT 3ft (1m)
SPREAD 3ft (1m)
SITE Full sun or partial shade
SOIL Fertile, moist but free-draining
HARDINESS Z3–8 H8–1
FLOWERING Summer

Panicum virgatum 'Heavy Metal' Blue switch grass

P

NATIVE TO NORTH AMERICAN PRAIRIES, there are several outstanding types of *Panicum virgatum*. 'Heavy Metal' is graceful with almost vertical, strappy leaves, about 24in (60cm) high, that are tinged blue and turn yellow in the autumn. Light, airy flowers crest the top of the leaves. 'Prairie Sky' is slightly bluer but tends to flop after a heavy downpour, while 'Hänse Herms' (red switch grass) becomes progressively redder over summer. Switch grass grows well in most gardens, but won't tolerate either wet or dry extremes. Also, choose the planting position with care and, if possible, site it where the flowers will stand out against a dark background.

OTHER VARIETY *P. virgatum* 'Rehbraun' (burgundy red foliage).

PLANT PROFILE

HEIGHT 4ft (1.2m)

SPREAD 30in (75cm)

SITE Full sun

SOIL Moist but free-draininng

HARDINESS Z5–9 H9–1

FLOWERING Early autumn

Use a trowel to carefully lift self-sown seedlings, each with its own root ball, from around the parent plant, and replant in any convenient gaps.

P

Papaver orientale 'Mrs. Perry' Oriental poppy

FORMING SMALL, SUBSTANTIAL CLUMPS, these poppies have hairy stems, leaves up to 12in (30cm) long, and buds that start to appear in late spring. These grow larger and larger until the flowers pop out and, at 6in (15cm) across, they really grab the eye. 'Mrs. Perry' is a soft salmon pink, but there are louder colors, such as the bright red 'Beauty of Livermere' with a black blotch like a huge bumblebee hiding in the base of the flower. Each flower lasts about three days, but more open in succession.

OTHER VARIETIES *P. orientale* 'Allegro' (orange-scarlet flowers); *P. orientale* 'Perry's White' (white flowers with maroon-purple centers); *P. orientale* 'Picotée' (white flowers with frilly orange-pink margins).

PLANT PROFILE

HEIGHT 18–36in (45–90cm)

SPREAD 24–36in (60–90cm)

SITE Full sun

SOIL Fertile, free-draining

HARDINESS Z4–9 H9–1

FLOWERING Late spring to midsummer

Paradisea liliastrum Paradise lily

P

NOT AS POPULAR TODAY as it once was, *Paradisea liliastrum* imparts a lilylike touch to the garden when its trumpet-shaped, scented white flowers open above grassy leaves in late spring. Not very tall, it is best given a position toward the front of a border or near shrubs, and needs to be planted in rich, moist but free-draining soil. The paradise lily can be difficult to find, but once it's established in the garden it should develop into a good-sized clump. Divide it in autumn to provide extra plants, and keep an eye out for attacks from slugs and snails.

OTHER VARIETY *P. lusitanica* (larger-growing, white flowers).

PLANT PROFILE

HEIGHT 12–24in (30–60cm)

SPREAD 12in (30cm)

SITE Sun or light shade

SOIL Moist, fertile, free-draining

HARDINESS Z7–9

FLOWERING Late spring or early summer

Parahebe perfoliata Digger's speedwell

THIS SPREADING EVERGREEN from Australia has floppy, wiry stems, with blue-green leaves and violet-blue flowers. It thrives in poor soil with good drainage, and can be grown in soil-filled cracks in walls, in rock or gravel gardens, or near the front of a border. There are several good alternatives, including the shrubby *Parahebe catarractae* 'Delight', with red-veined violet-blue flowers. They all combine well, but digger's speedwell is one of the tallest. Avoid a position where it is exposed to cold, drying winds.

OTHER VARIETIES *P.* x *bidwillii* 'Kea' (smaller-growing, crimson-veined white flowers); *P. catarractae* (smaller-growing, purple-veined white flowers); *P. lyallii* (smaller-growing, blue flowers).

PLANT PROFILE	
HEIGHT 24–30in (60–75cm)	
SPREAD 18in (45cm)	
SITE Full sun	
SOIL Poor, free-draining	
HARDINESS Z9–11 H12–3	
FLOWERING Late summer	

Pennisetum orientale Oriental fountain grass

DISTINCTIVE BOTTLEBRUSH-LIKE FLOWERS emerging from beautiful, arching foliage on top of long, thin stems are the key features of this plant. From a distance the flowers look as if they are covered in tiny pieces of cotton batting and add a soft touch to a gravel garden or a border. It is slightly tender and needs a warm, sheltered site, and soil with very good drainage. Leave the stems standing over winter to add shape and structure to the garden at this time of year, and cut them back in early spring before the new growth begins.

OTHER VARIETIES *P. alopecuroides* 'Hameln' (larger-growing, greenish white flowers, golden yellow autumn leaves); *P. macrourum* (smaller-growing, pale green, bristly flowers).

P

PLANT PROFILE
HEIGHT 24in (60cm)
SPREAD 30in (75cm)
SITE Full sun
SOIL Free-draining
HARDINESS Z6–9 H9–1
FLOWERING Mid- and late summer

P

Penstemon 'Pennington Gem' Beardtongue

PROLIFIC AND EASY TO GROW, penstemons perform throughout the summer and are terrific garden value. They come in white, purple, red, pink, mauve, blue, and even yellow, most with a white throat. 'Pennington Gem' has typical, downward-pointing tubular flowers held on stiff, upright stems, and can be used virtually anywhere in the border. In colder zones it needs a warm, sunny garden position, and free-draining, fertile soil. Cuttings taken in summer quickly root and guarantee plants for the following year.

OTHER VARIETIES *P.* 'Alice Hindley' (larger-growing, lilac-blue flowers); *P.* 'Apple Blossom' (smaller-growing, pale pink flowers); *P.* 'Sour Grapes' (smaller-growing, grayish blue flowers).

PLANT PROFILE

HEIGHT 30in (75cm)

SPREAD 18in (45cm)

SITE Full sun

SOIL Fertile, free-draining

HARDINESS Z6–9 H9–6

FLOWERING Midsummer to midautumn

Pentaglottis sempervirens Green alkanet

P

THINK CAREFULLY before acquiring this plant, because once it is in your garden it can be extremely difficult to eradicate. It self-seeds, and if any slivers of its deep root are left when you are attempting to dig it out, they will regrow. Nonetheless, it makes very effective groundcover for a shady site, and has leaves up to 16in (40cm) long and bright blue flowers like those of a forget-me-not (*Myosotis*). The best place for green alkanet is a wild or woodland garden, where the soil is moist and rich and it can spread at will. To keep the plant from self-seeding, shear it as soon as the flowers start to fade.

PLANT PROFILE

HEIGHT 28–40in (70–100cm)

SPREAD 28–40in (70–100cm)

SITE Partial or deep shade

SOIL Moist, fertile

HARDINESS Z6–9

FLOWERING Spring to early summer

P

Persicaria affinis 'Donald Lowndes' Knotweed

KNOTWEED IS A LOW-KEY PLANT, great for filling gaps in a border or providing groundcover. More suitable for a border, 'Donald Lowndes' is distinguished by short spikes of pale pink flowers, held up like candles above the leaves. It needs moist soil, but if you have free-draining conditions, try *Persicaria bisorta* instead. Other good varieties include 'Darjeeling Red', which initially has pink flowers that darken to red, and 'Superba', with its deep pinkish red blooms that become redder as the summer progresses.

OTHER VARIETIES *P. amplexicaulis* (taller, bright red to purple or white flowers); *P. bistorta* 'Superba' (taller, soft pink flowers); *P. campanulata* (taller, fragrant, pink or white flowers); *P. milletii* (taller, crimson flowers).

PLANT PROFILE

HEIGHT 8in (20cm)

SPREAD 12in (30cm)

SITE Full sun or partial shade

SOIL Moist

HARDINESS Z3–8 H8–1

FLOWERING Midsummer to midautumn

Phalaris arundinacea var. *picta* 'Picta' Gardener's garters

P

SOMETIMES KNOWN AS RIBBON GRASS, if this plant is allowed the space to roam in a wild garden, near a natural pond, or even right up to the water's edge, it makes a wonderful sight—especially in late spring and early summer. It needs to be planted with care, however, because in rich, moist soil it can be very invasive. The evergreen foliage has fresh green and white stripes, and it should be sheared after flowering to provide a second flush of leaves. This also prevents the plants from reverting to all-green foliage.

OTHER VARIETY *P. arundinacea* var. *picta* 'Feesey' (purplish blue flowers, light green leaves with white stripes, stem bases flushed pink).

PLANT PROFILE

HEIGHT 3ft (1m)

SPREAD Indefinite

SITE Full sun or partial shade

SOIL Moist

HARDINESS Z4–9 H9–1

FLOWERING Early and midsummer

P | *Phlomis russeliana* Sticky Jerusalem sage

INTERESTING AND UNUSUAL-LOOKING, this perennial has circular clusters of hooded, pale yellow flowers spaced out at intervals up its vertical stems. Although it doesn't make a powerful color statement in the garden, it adds a quirky surprise. It grows in most situations, provided it has average, free-draining soil, and, like most phlomis, it is just about drought-tolerant. This makes it an ideal candidate for a gravel garden or a dry, sunny border. The seedheads add an extra dimension of interest in winter.

OTHER VARIETY *P. bovei* subsp. *maroccana* (larger-growing, purple-pink flowers with purple spots inside the petals, white-woolly outside, gray-green leaves).

PLANT PROFILE

HEIGHT To 3ft (1m)

SPREAD 30in (75cm)

SITE Full sun or light shade

SOIL Average, free-draining

HARDINESS Z4–9 H9–1

FLOWERING Late spring to early autumn

With all phlox species, as soon as the blooms start to fade, cut back the spent flower stems to neaten up the plant and encourage more flowering sideshoots to develop.

Phlox paniculata 'Starfire' Perennial phlox

P

THESE SHOWY BORDER PLANTS have an eye-catching domed head of flowers in a wide range of colors. They are best grown in sizable groups to provide a wafting sweet scent in the early evening. Use the same colors together or the effect can become spotty. 'Starfire' is at the hot-hued end of the spectrum, and contrasts well with 'White Admiral' or 'Blue Boy'. Good pastels include pale lilac 'Prospero' and pale pink 'Sandringham'. Average garden soil is fine, with well-rotted compost forked in. For extra flowers, deadhead throughout summer.

OTHER VARIETIES *P. paniculata* 'Brigadier' (pinkish red flowers); *P. paniculata* 'Fujiyama' (white flowers); *P. paniculata* 'Le Mahdi' (bluish purple flowers); *P. paniculata* 'Windsor' (reddish pink flowers).

PLANT PROFILE

HEIGHT 3ft (1m)

SPREAD 18in (45cm)

SITE Full sun or partial shade

SOIL Average, free-draining

HARDINESS Z4–8 H8–1

FLOWERING Summer to early or midautumn

P | *Phormium tenax* New Zealand flax

THE SWORDLIKE, EVERGREEN LEAVES of this striking plant are up to 10ft (3m) high, while the summer flower spikes, bearing dull red flowers, tower above them. Use it as a focal feature in a gravel or Mediterranean-style garden, or in a large pot. Add a thick layer of mulch around the base of the plant in winter or, if growing in a pot, move it to a warm spot. Divide plants every three years, keeping an outer section with leaves and roots—established plants may be impossible to dig up.

OTHER VARIETIES *P. cookianum* subsp. *hookeri* 'Tricolor' (smaller, yellow-green flowers, leaves with cream and red margins); *P.* 'Sundowner' (smaller, bronze-green leaves with pink margins).

PLANT PROFILE

HEIGHT 12ft (4m)

SPREAD 6ft (2m)

SITE Full sun

SOIL Fertile, free-draining

HARDINESS Z9–11 H12–6

FLOWERING Summer

Phragmites australis subsp. *australis* 'Variegatus' Common reed

P

IF YOU HAVE A BOG GARDEN, very large pond, or streamside bank you can take on this invasive perennial. It can stand in water up to 5ft (1.5m) deep, where it provides an effective hiding place for wild fowl. (The nonvariegated *Phragmites australis* is even more invasive and requires a lake.) The sturdy, upright, yellow-striped leaves grow 24in (60cm) long, and are topped by superb, 18in- (45cm-) long flowers held on even taller stems. The plumes are smaller than, but similar to, those of pampas grass (*Cortaderia selloana*), and make a magnificent sight when ruffled by the wind. An effective way of restricting the spread of 'Variegatus' is to grow it in a large underwater container.

PLANT PROFILE

HEIGHT 8ft (2.5m)

SPREAD Indefinite

SITE Full sun

SOIL Wet

HARDINESS Z5–9 H9–4

FLOWERING Late summer to midautumn

P

Phuopsis stylosa Crosswort

THIS SUMMER–LONG–FLOWERING PERENNIAL needs to be grown at the foot of a wall or close to a path so that it can flop over and blur any straight edges with its straggling stems. It can even be used as groundcover on banks. Flowers are funnel-shaped and fragrant, and its leaves are narrow and grow in whorls. By cutting the plant back in the autumn, after flowering, it will become more compact and shapely. Grow this pale pink form with 'Purpurea' which has much richer pink flowers. Both retain their leaves through the autumn, and even into winter, until the temperatures start to dive. The soil needs to be free-draining.

PLANT PROFILE

HEIGHT 6in (15cm)

SPREAD 20in (50cm)

SITE Full sun or partial shade

SOIL Free-draining

HARDINESS Z5–8 H8–5

FLOWERING Summer

Physalis alkekengi var. *franchetii* Chinese lantern

P

THE BEST REASON for growing this plant is the amazing seedheads, not the creamy white flowers that really don't amount to anything much. The seedheads look like small, red paper balls or lanterns (botanically known as calyces), with bright orange-scarlet berries within, and are used for cut-flower displays. The berries are edible, but eating any other part of the plant could give you an upset stomach. Extremely tolerant of a wide range of growing conditions, Chinese lanterns are happy in most gardens and require average soil that never becomes waterlogged or bakes dry. Wear gloves when handling the leaves because direct contact can irritate the skin.

OTHER VARIETY *P. alkekengi* (red lanterns).

PLANT PROFILE

HEIGHT 24–30in (60–75cm)

SPREAD 3ft (1m)

SITE Full sun or partial shade

SOIL Average, free-draining

HARDINESS Z4–8

FLOWERING Midsummer

P

Physostegia virginiana var. *speciosa* 'Variegata' Obedient plant

A USEFUL COMPANION PLANT with a good show of flowers held on stiffly upright stems, this plant get its common name from the fact that when the flowers are nudged to one side, they do not bounce back. The plant makes a good-sized clump of variegated foliage, and provides plenty of magenta-pink flowers for cutting from the middle of summer to early autumn. To do well it needs moist, rich soil and, in ideal conditions, it will spread. 'Vivid' has stronger-colored, bright purple-pink flowers.

OTHER VARIETIES *P. virginiana* 'Bouquet Rose' (pale lilac-pink flowers); *P. virginiana* 'Summer Snow' (white and green flowers).

PLANT PROFILE
HEIGHT To 4ft (1.2m)
SPREAD 24in (60cm) or more
SITE Full sun or partial shade
SOIL Moist, fertile
HARDINESS Z4–8 H8–1
FLOWERING Midsummer to early autumn

Phytolacca americana Pokeweed

P

TALL, INVASIVE, AND VERY POISONOUS, pokeweed is a candidate for the wild garden, light woodland, or even a streamside setting. The small white to pink flowers are followed by pokeweed's best feature—toxic, strikingly colored, blackish maroon berries. Despite the health warnings, it does make an impressive plant, large enough to become a hedgelike summer barrier; in the autumn, the foliage reddens up. All parts cause severe discomfort if eaten, and it should be kept out of gardens where children might be tempted by the berries, which can be lethal.

OTHER VARIETY *P. polyandra* (smaller-growing, purple-pink flowers, toxic black berries, leaves turn yellow in autumn).

PLANT PROFILE

HEIGHT To 12ft (4m)

SPREAD 3ft (1m)

SITE Full sun or partial shade

SOIL Moist, fertile

HARDINESS Z5–9 H9–5

FLOWERING Midsummer to early autumn

P

Platycodon grandiflorus Balloon flower

THE WAY THE FLOWER BUDS SWELL and swell, getting rounder and fatter until they open, gives this plant its common name of balloon flower. The flowers are 2in (5cm) wide, with dark blue veins and pointed tips, while the stems are not entirely sturdy, and need staking to keep them upright. Provide rich, free-draining soil that does not dry out and bake in summer. *Platycodon* 'Mariesii' is a shorter, dark blue balloon flower that does not require staking.

OTHER VARIETIES *P. grandiflorus albus* (blue-veined white flowers); *P. grandiflorus* 'Apoyama' (deep violet flowers); *P. grandiflorus* 'Park's Double Blue' (double violet-blue flowers); *P. grandiflorus* 'Perlmutterschale' (pale pink flowers).

PLANT PROFILE
HEIGHT To 24in (60cm)
SPREAD 12in (30cm)
SITE Full sun or partial shade
SOIL Fertile, free-draining
HARDINESS Z4–9 H9–1
FLOWERING Late summer

Polemonium 'Lambrook Mauve' Jacob's ladder

P

THESE COTTAGE-GARDEN FAVORITES have a delicate quality, with flowers in lilac, blue, purple, pink, yellow, or white. The taller forms can be grown in borders, the shorter ones in rock or gravel gardens. Lilac-blue 'Lambrook Mauve' is an ideal choice for an informal bed, and needs average soil with well-rotted compost added to it to keep the ground moist. Deadhead promptly when the blooms have faded to eliminate seedlings and prolong the flowering season.

OTHER VARIETIES *P. caeruleum* (larger-growing, lavender-blue flowers); *P. caeruleum* subsp. *caeruleum* f. *album* (white flowers); *P. carneum* (smaller-growing, pale pink or yellow flowers); *P. pauciflorum* (red-tinted pale yellow flowers).

PLANT PROFILE
HEIGHT To 18in (45cm)
SPREAD To 18in (45cm)
SITE Full sun or partial shade
SOIL Average, moist
HARDINESS Z4–8 H8–1
FLOWERING Late spring and early summer

Polygonatum x *hybridum* 'Striatum' Solomon's seal

ONE OF THE BEST SPRING PLANTS, Solomon's seal hides itself away in shady corners or borders, where each long, arching stem is adorned with a row of small, green-lipped, white, pendent flowers. These are followed by tiny, blue-black berries. The leaves feature thin white stripes. Like other polygonatums, 'Striatum' spreads well to form attractive clumps where there is plenty of moist, rich soil. The flower stems can be cut for indoor displays.

OTHER VARIETIES *P. hookeri* (smaller-growing, pink flowers, black berries); *P. humile* (smaller-growing, white flowers, blue-black berries); *P. multiflorum* (smaller-growing, green-tipped white flowers, black berries); *P. odoratum* 'Flore Pleno' (double, green-tipped white flowers).

PLANT PROFILE
HEIGHT To 5ft (1.5m)
SPREAD 12in (30cm)
SITE Full or partial shade
SOIL Moist, fertile
HARDINESS Z6–9
FLOWERING Late spring

CUCKOO SPIT

Blobs of frothy liquid on stems are the protective covering of small green insects. These usually do no harm and should be picked off by hand.

Potentilla 'Gibson's Scarlet' Cinquefoil

P

BRIGHT TOMATO RED flowers add impact to any hot color scheme. First come the rounded leaves, like those of a strawberry, then the flat circular blooms the size of small coins, which keep appearing all summer on top of wiry, scrambling stems. It makes a vibrant show when planted next to a taller, wider, yellow-flowering potentilla, and also stands out next to a small, silver-beige grass. Average garden soil is fine; dig plenty of sand into heavy ground to improve drainage.

OTHER VARIETIES *P. aurea* (smaller-growing, golden yellow flowers); *P. erecta* (smaller-growing, yellow flowers); *P.* 'Etna' (velvety red flowers); *P.* 'Gloire de Nancy' (double, reddish orange flowers); *P.* 'Monsieur Rouillard' (blood red flowers with yellow marks).

PLANT PROFILE

HEIGHT To 18in (45cm)

SPREAD 24in (60cm)

SITE Full sun

SOIL Average, free-draining

HARDINESS Z4–7 H7–1

FLOWERING Early to late summer

P | *Primula beesiana* Candelabra primula

ELEGANT AND EYE-CATCHING, this primula has a few long leaves at the base and a tall, thin, summer-flowering stem rising out of them. Dozens of tiny, bright reddish purple flowers, each with a yellow eye, appear in clusters right up to the top. It needs moist, rich, neutral to acidic soil (the type you would find in bog gardens), and will tolerate a sunny position provided the soil never dries out. The best time to divide established plants is in the spring.

OTHER VARIETIES *P. anisodora* (green-eyed brown-purple flowers); *P. aurantiaca* (smaller-growing, red-orange flowers); *P. bulleyana* (crimson flowers); *P. burmanica* (yellow-eyed red-purple flowers); *P.* 'Inverewe' (brilliant red flowers); *P. pulverulenta* (red-purple flowers).

PLANT PROFILE	
HEIGHT 24in (60cm)	
SPREAD 24in (60cm)	
SITE Partial shade	
SOIL Moist, fertile	
HARDINESS Z5–8	
FLOWERING Summer	

Primula florindae Giant cowslip

P

THIS SUPERB PLANT is really worth growing, but you must provide it with wet ground throughout the year, making it an obvious candidate for a bog garden or the damp ground beside a stream. The flowering stems rise up out of the lush leaves and carry long-lasting clusters of about forty pale yellow flowers. They are excellent for picking for an indoor display, where their gentle scent can be better appreciated. A sunny garden position is suitable only if the soil is moist throughout the year. Only a couple of plants are needed because they soon spread, forming magnificent clumps.

PLANT PROFILE

HEIGHT To 4ft (1.2m)

SPREAD 3ft (1m)

SITE Partial shade

SOIL Moist, fertile

HARDINESS Z3–8 H8–1

FLOWERING Summer

P | *Primula vialii*

LOOKING LIKE A MINIATURE KNIPHOFIA (and often called the red-hot poker primula), this is a highly attractive and distinctive plant. It initially has a two-tone cone on top of a short flower stem. From a distance, it looks as though the cone is bearing two different-colored flowers—blue and red. In fact, it is the buds that are red, and in early summer they open from the bottom of the cone to reveal tiny blue flowers. Since it has a reputation for being short-lived, collect seed after flowering, and then make sure the young seedlings are well watered. *Primula vialii* is suitable for bog gardens or the damp soil beside a stream.

PLANT PROFILE

HEIGHT 12–24in (30–60cm)

SPREAD 12in (30cm)

SITE Partial shade

SOIL Moist, fertile

HARDINESS Z5–8 H8–5

FLOWERING Summer

Prunella grandiflora 'Pink Loveliness' Self-heal

P

THE BEST POSSIBLE USE of 'Pink Loveliness' is as groundcover. It grows to form a thick covering of 4in- (10cm-) long leaves and, in summer, produces clear pink flowers on upright stems. The major advantage of this plant is that it will grow just about anywhere, from sunny to shady sites. It self-seeds unless sheared as the flowers start to fade. Don't confuse it with the blue-purple *Prunella vulgaris*, which is grown in herb gardens and was traditionally used to heal external injuries and other ailments.

OTHER VARIETY   *P. grandiflora* 'White Loveliness' (pure white flowers).

PLANT PROFILE

HEIGHT 6in (15cm)

SPREAD 3ft (1m)

SITE Full sun or partial shade

SOIL Average

HARDINESS Z5–8 H8–5

FLOWERING Summer

P

Pulmonaria 'Lewis Palmer' Lungwort

WITH ITS PINK FLOWERS in early spring that gradually turn bright
blue, and its long, white-spotted leaves, this plant has two attractions.
The leaves can grow up to 12in (30cm) long and fully develop after
the plant has stopped flowering. It needs to be grown in light or
deep shade in moist, rich soil, and makes good groundcover for a
site close to deciduous trees. There is a wide choice of lungworts,
some with white flowers (*Pulmonaria saccharata* 'Sissinghurst White'),
others with red blooms (*P. rubra* 'Redstart').

OTHER VARIETIES *P. angustifolia* (rich blue flowers); *P.* 'Margery Fish'
(smaller-growing, coral-pink flowers turning violet); *P. rubra* 'Bowles' Red'
(coral-red flowers); *P. saccharata* 'Leopard' (red, pink-tinted flowers).

PLANT PROFILE

HEIGHT 35cm (14in)

SPREAD 18in (45cm)

SITE Light or deep shade

SOIL Moist, fertile

HARDINESS Z5–8 H8–5

FLOWERING Early spring

ROOT CUTTINGS

Lift a vigorous plant. Cut a thick, healthy root close to the crown, and then slice into 2in (5cm) sections. Insert the roots vertically into pots of moist potting mix. The top ends of each cutting must be level with the surface.

Pulsatilla vulgaris Pasque flower

P

ATTRACTIVE PURPLE FLOWERS, some white, held on short stems provide a fine spring show. The plant's requirement for excellent drainage and its diminutive size make it ideal for raised beds, a rock or gravel garden, the front of a border, or troughs. The silky flowers have an open bell shape with a yellow eye, and are followed in the summer by attractive seedheads. The white form is *Pulsatilla vulgaris alba*, 'Barton's Pink' is pink, and 'Röde Klokke' a deep red. Give each plant some space because it will grow to form a good-sized clump.

OTHER VARIETIES *P. halleri* (lavender-blue flowers); *P. vernalis* (smaller-growing, white flowers tinted bluish violet).

PLANT PROFILE

HEIGHT 4–8in (10–20cm)

SPREAD 8in (20cm)

SITE Full sun

SOIL Free-draining

HARDINESS Z5–7 H7–5

FLOWERING Spring

R | *Ranunculus ficaria* 'Brazen Hussy' Lesser celandine

THIS TERRIFIC LITTLE BUTTERCUP has shiny brown leaves that offset the brash, bright yellow flowers. It grows naturally in woodland conditions, where the soil is moist and rich and the light varies from dappled sun to partial shade. 'Brazen Hussy' catches the eye when seen against gravel, where the full contrast between leaf and flower color stands out, but it is also happy growing in wilder parts of the garden. Like most buttercups, it spreads well.

OTHER VARIETIES *R. acris* 'Flore Pleno' (larger-growing, double, yellow flowers); *R. bulbosus* 'F. M. Burton' (larger-growing, creamy yellow flowers in autumn); *R. ficaria* 'Collarette' (double, yellow flowers, leaves with bronze bands); *R. gramineus* (larger-growing, lemon yellow flowers).

PLANT PROFILE

HEIGHT 2in (5cm)

SPREAD 12in (30cm)

SITE Partial shade

SOIL Moist, fertile

HARDINESS Z4–8 H8–1

FLOWERING Early spring

Rehmannia elata Chinese foxglove

R

THE TUBULAR FLOWERS of this appropriately named plant look like those of a foxglove. This bushy perennial has dark green, 8in- (20cm-) long leaves, and in late spring and early summer vertical spires with flowers up to 4in (10cm) long. It needs a sunny, frost-free site and free-draining soil; in cooler regions, it is best to lift the plant in autumn, cut it back, and pot it for overwintering in a cool greenhouse. Water the plant periodically to prevent the soil from drying out completely, and put it outside again the following spring, after the last frost.

OTHER VARIETY *R. glutinosa* (smaller-growing, reddish brown flowers with pale yellow-brown lips).

PLANT PROFILE
HEIGHT 5ft (1.5m)
SPREAD 20in (50cm)
SITE Full sun
SOIL Free-draining
HARDINESS Z12–15 H12–10
FLOWERING Late spring to midsummer

R | *Rheum palmatum* 'Atrosanguineum' Chinese rhubarb

THIS IS A SPECIAL PLANT for a special place in the garden. In spring, the new, dramatic, rhubarblike, jagged leaves are reddish purple, and fade gradually to dark green. They're wonderfully large, reaching 3ft (1m) in length, and are accompanied by the vertical flower spikes, which are almost as impressive, with sprays of tiny crimson flowers. It makes a magnificent sight in moist soil by a pond, but remember when placing this plant that it starts to die down in late summer and will need something nearby to keep the show going.

OTHER VARIETIES *R.* 'Ace of Hearts' (smaller-growing, pale pink to white flowers, red- and purple-veined leaves); *R. palmatum* (creamy green to deep red flowers).

PLANT PROFILE

HEIGHT To 8ft (2.5m)

SPREAD To 6ft (2m)

SITE Full sun or partial shade

SOIL Moist, fertile

HARDINESS Z5–9 H9–5

FLOWERING Early summer

Rhodiola rosea Roseroot

R

MAKING AN IMPRESSIVE FLOWERING CLUMP, which attracts bees and butterflies, roseroot also has very attractive foliage. The leaves are almost oval and pointed, fleshy and bluish gray, growing all the way up each strong stem, while the yellow flowers, with just a hint of green, are held at the very top. It is a good plant for a rock garden, or at the front of a raised bed or border, where it will be remarkably free-flowering. Avoid shade and heavy clay soil, and water it well in dry summer spells.

OTHER VARIETY *R. heterodonta* (larger-growing, star-shaped yellow flowers from red buds, male flowers with red or purple-red centers, grayish green leaves).

PLANT PROFILE

HEIGHT 2–12in (5–30cm)

SPREAD 8in (20cm)

SITE Full sun

SOIL Fertile

HARDINESS Z1–6 H6–1

FLOWERING Summer

R *Rodgersia pinnata* 'Superba' Featherleaf Rodgers flower

THIS PLANT HAS PLENTY OF IMPACT. It unfurls magnificent leaves, reaching up to 3ft (1m) long, that are bronze on opening in the spring, gradually turning dark green. In the summer they are topped by erect stems holding fluffy flowers that stay in good condition until midautumn. For the best display, plant it in moist, rich soil, out of the midsummer sun, and sheltered from winds. In a sunny site, use a thick mulch of compost to keep in the soil moisture. The new bronze foliage makes an effective contrast in a moist gravel bed.

OTHER VARIETIES *R. aesculifolia* (larger-growing, white or pink flowers); *R. podophylla* (larger-growing, creamy green flowers, leaves bronze when young, bronze-red in autumn.

PLANT PROFILE
HEIGHT 4ft (1.2m)
SPREAD 30in (75cm)
SITE Sun or semishade
SOIL Moist, fertile
HARDINESS Z3–7 H7–1
FLOWERING Mid- and late summer

Rudbeckia 'Herbstonne' Coneflower

R

As HIGH-IMPACT SUMMER PLANTS for a border, coneflowers are ideal. 'Herbstonne' has large, bright yellow, daisylike blooms with a brown cone in the middle. It makes a substantial clump and needs plenty of space. If it is too tall for your liking, you can pinch out the growing tips when the plant reaches about 30in (75cm) high. In windy gardens, staking may be necessary. Add a thick spring mulch of compost and water in dry weather to prevent plants from becoming floppy. A shorter alternative is the similar *Rudbeckia fulgida* var. *sullivantii* 'Goldsturm' (black-eyed Susan).

OTHER VARIETIES *R. fulgida* var. *deamii* (shorter, orange-yellow flowers); *R. hirta* (shorter, golden yellow flowers).

PLANT PROFILE
HEIGHT 6ft (2m)
SPREAD 3ft (1m)
SITE Full sun or partial shade
SOIL Fertile, free-draining
HARDINESS Z3–9 H9–1
FLOWERING Midsummer to early autumn

S

Saccharum ravennae Ravenna grass

MAKING A SPECTACULAR SIGHT, this grass from the Mediterranean and North Africa has swordlike leaves that grow to about 3ft (1m) high, and have a tendency to arch over. Bursting out of the clumps of foliage are huge flower spikes topped by feathery plumes, which initially have a pink tinge before turning silver. A good flower display does depend on a long, hot summer, however, and the soil should be average, rather than rich, and free-draining. It will grow just about anywhere in the garden—from borders to gravel gardens, or as a feature in its own special bed in a lawn—as long as it receives full sun. In colder regions, protect the crown of the plant in winter with horticultural fleece or a thick layer of mulch.

PLANT PROFILE
HEIGHT 6–10ft (2–3m)
SPREAD 4ft (1.2m)
SITE Full sun
SOIL Average, free-draining
HARDINESS Z6–9 H9–6
FLOWERING Late summer and autumn

Salvia patens

SUNNY BORDERS ARE ENHANCED by the rich, flamboyant colors and pale pastels of summer-flowering salvias. The deep blue *Salvia patens* is for the front of a border, while a taller, pale blue type is *S. uliginosa*, at 6ft (2m); *S. guaranitica* is nearly as tall with dark blue flowers. All need a sheltered site in full sun, good drainage, and a mulch of compost in colder areas.

OTHER VARIETIES *S. buchananii* (magenta-red flowers); *S. involucrata* (larger-growing, purplish red flowers); *S. patens* 'Cambridge Blue' (pale blue flowers); *S. splendens* 'Red Riches' (smaller-growing, scarlet flowers); *S.* x *superba* (larger-growing, bright violet or purple flowers).

PLANT PROFILE
HEIGHT 18–24in (45–60cm)
SPREAD 18–24in (45–60cm)
SITE Full sun
SOIL Free-draining
HARDINESS Z8–9 H9–8
FLOWERING Midsummer to midautumn

S

Salvia x *sylvestris* 'Mainacht'

THIS HARDY SALVIA makes a colorful, bushy plant and is covered with indigo blue flowers throughout the summer, making it a good gap-filler for the front of a border, or a gravel garden. Alternatives include 'Rose Queen', which is rose pink, while *Salvia* x *superba* is very similar to the different types of *S.* x *sylvestris* and equally hardy, with flowers in violet or purple. All need free-draining soil and full sun—avoid soil that's too rich, since this encourages them to produce more leaves than flowers.

OTHER VARIETIES *S. nemorosa* 'Ostfriesland' (smaller-growing, deep blue-violet flowers); *S.* x *sylvestris* 'Blauhügel' (smaller-growing, pure blue flowers); *S.* x *sylvestris* 'Rose Queen' (rose pink flowers).

PLANT PROFILE	
HEIGHT 28in (70cm)	
SPREAD 18in (45cm)	
SITE Full sun	
SOIL Average, free-draining	
HARDINESS Z4–7 H7–3	
FLOWERING Early and midsummer	

Sanguisorba obtusa Burnet

S

IF GARDEN SPACE IS TIGHT and you don't have room or the warm conditions for a large callistemon, then try this smaller perennial, which has beautiful, bottlebrush-like flowers. The flower spikes are 3in (8cm) long and held well clear of the bright, fresh green leaves. It is easy to grow, provided the soil is fertile and free-draining but never dries out. It has a long flowering season and deserves a prominent position toward the front of a border or by a pond. Divide clumps in early spring to make more plants.

OTHER VARIETIES *S. canadensis* (larger-growing, spikes of fluffy white flowers); *S. officinalis* (larger-growing, dense spikes of small red-brown flowers).

PLANT PROFILE
HEIGHT To 24in (60cm)
SPREAD To 24in (60cm)
SITE Full sun or partial shade
SOIL Fertile, moist but free-draining
HARDINESS Z4–7 H8–3
FLOWERING Mid- or late summer to early autumn

S

Saponaria ocymoides Tumbling Ted

THE TOP OF A STONE WALL is perfect for this plant; its small pink summer flowers will tumble down the sides and show it off to the best effect. Its preference for free-draining conditions also makes it suitable for rock gardens, but beware of its quick-spreading habit. If it's too vigorous, then try the red 'Rubra Compacta', which has a neater habit, or the white 'Alba'. They can all be cut back after flowering to restrict their spread, and to keep the plants neat.

OTHER VARIETIES *S.* 'Bressingham' (deep pink flowers); *S. officinalis* (larger-growing, pink, red, or white flowers); *S. officinalis* 'Alba Plena' (double, white flowers); *S. x olivana* (smaller-growing, pale pink flowers).

PLANT PROFILE	
HEIGHT 3in (8cm)	
SPREAD 18in (45cm)	
SITE Full sun	
SOIL Free-draining	
HARDINESS Z4–8 H8–1	
FLOWERING Summer	

Scabiosa atropurpurea 'Chile Black' Pincushion flower

S

COMBINING WELL WITH silver-leaved plants, bright green leaves, and flashy red dahlias, 'Chile Black' has small, dark red flowers (looking almost black from a distance) with white flecks. Grow it in an average soil with excellent drainage in a border or a gravel garden where the stones provide a foil for its dark flowers. Although short-lived, *Scabiosa atropurpurea* 'Ace of Spades' is a fine alternative with equally deep crimson flowers, blooming well into winter in mild-climate gardens.

OTHER VARIETIES *S.* 'Butterfly Blue' (smaller-growing, lavender-blue flowers); *S. caucasica* 'Miss Wilmott' (larger-growing, white flowers); *S. graminifolia* 'Pinkushion' (smaller-growing, rose pink flowers).

PLANT PROFILE	
HEIGHT 24in (60cm)	
SPREAD 24in (60cm)	
SITE Full sun	
SOIL Average, free-draining	
HARDINESS Z1–11	
FLOWERING Mid- and late summer	

S *Schoenoplectus lacustris* subsp. *tabernaemontani* 'Zebrinus' Club-rush

THIS TYPE OF BULRUSH is for boggy, moist, neutral to acidic soil at the edge of a large pond, lake, or stream. 'Zebrinus' has upright, graceful, thin, gray green stems, with highly distinctive horizontal creamy white bands that make it among the most spectacular of the rushes. The brown flowers are insignificant. Note that this rush is sometimes listed as *Scirpus* instead of *Schoenoplectus*. Other excellent varieties include the virtually white-stemmed 'Albescens' and the yellow-stemmed 'Golden Spears'.

PLANT PROFILE
HEIGHT 3ft (1m)
SPREAD 24in (60cm)
SITE Full sun
SOIL Wet
HARDINESS Z6–9 H9–6
FLOWERING Early to late summer

Scrophularia auriculata 'Variegata' Water figwort

S

A PRIME CONTENDER FOR BOG GARDENS, the shallows of a pond, or very moist borders, 'Variegata' has attractive leaves with broad, creamy white margins. Since the flowers are not particularly exciting, you can remove the flower stems and allow the plant to put all its energy into more leaf production, or cut them off the moment they start to fade. 'Variegata' can be grown among the likes of *Myosotis* (water forget-me-nots) and *Lysichiton americanus* (skunk cabbage). If you are growing it in the shallows of a pond, it likes to be planted at a depth of about 6in (15cm).

OTHER VARIETY *S. auriculata* (yellowish green flowers, wrinkled, toothed, dark green leaves).

PLANT PROFILE
HEIGHT 3ft (1m)
SPREAD 3ft (1m)
SITE Dappled to partial shade
SOIL Wet
HARDINESS Z5–9 H9–5
FLOWERING Early summer to early autumn

S | *Sedum 'Herbstfreude'* Stonecrop

IMPARTING A VALUABLE DASH of pink, white, or purple flowers to the autumn garden, the taller sedums have the added bonus of attracting butterflies and bees. 'Herbstfreude' has deep pink flowers that gradually acquire a bronze tint, and end up dark copper-red. Sedums are succulents with attractive fleshy leaves, and can be grown in borders and around ponds, away from the moist edges, in average soil with good drainage. Divide them in the autumn, after flowering, by slicing off a section with some roots attached.

OTHER VARIETIES *S. spectabile* 'Brilliant' (smaller-growing, pink flowers); *S. telephium* subsp. *maximum* 'Atropurpureum' (pink flowers with orange centers); *S. telephium* 'Munstead Red' (red flowers).

PLANT PROFILE

HEIGHT 24in (60cm)

SPREAD 24in (60cm)

SITE Full sun

SOIL Average, free-draining

HARDINESS Z4–11 H12–1

FLOWERING Early autumn

Selinum wallichianum Himalayan parsley

COTTAGE GARDENS, INFORMAL BORDERS, and wild gardens are all excellent sites for this plant (which looks a little like cow parsley), although an immaculate formal border may not be the best position. The multibranched stems have fernlike leaves and are topped by tiny, star-shaped white flowers. Both the flowers and the foliage enliven cut-flower displays. In the wild, it is often found growing on rocky slopes and mountain meadows in Europe and the Himalayas, and needs similar good drainage and average soil in the garden. Be sure to find the perfect position when planting because it resents being moved once it is in the ground and established.

PLANT PROFILE

HEIGHT To 6ft (2m)

SPREAD 24in (60cm)

SITE Full sun or partial shade

SOIL Average, free-draining

HARDINESS Z4–7

FLOWERING Midsummer to early autumn

S | *Senecio pulcher* Showy groundsel

THIS IS A PLANT WITH A DIFFERENCE. Most senecios have yellow, daisylike flowers, but this South American species has sprays of almost magenta–mauve blooms with prominent yellow eyes, and is good enough to be the star plant in any group. It requires soil with good drainage, and it needs a sunny, sheltered position in the garden. In cold-climate gardens you can dig up *Senecio pulcher*, cut it back, and pot it for overwintering in a cool greenhouse.

OTHER VARIETIES   *S. smithii* (larger-growing, white flowers with yellow centers, moisture-loving); *S. tanguticus* (larger-growing, bright yellow flowers, invasive).

PLANT PROFILE
HEIGHT 18–24in (45–60cm)
SPREAD 20in (50cm)
SITE Full sun
SOIL Free-draining
HARDINESS Z11–15 H12–6
FLOWERING Mid- and late autumn

Sidalcea 'Elsie Heugh' Prairie mallow

S

LIKE A SHORTER VERSION of a hollyhock, 'Elsie Heugh' has open flowers ranged toward the top of vertical spires that tower above the foliage. The rich pink 'Elsie Heugh' is a gem for cottage gardens or formal borders, where it adds a gentle, summery note. Other colors are in the reddish pink to soft pink range. Sidalceas grow in most sunny gardens with fertile soil. Cut back the stems once the flowers are finished and you should be rewarded with a second flush of flowers toward autumn.

OTHER VARIETIES *S. candida* (smaller-growing, white or cream flowers); *S.* 'Croftway Red' (reddish pink flowers); *S.* 'William Smith' (deep rose pink flowers with salmon pink tints).

PLANT PROFILE
HEIGHT 3ft (1m)
SPREAD 18in (45cm)
SITE Full sun
SOIL Fertile, moist but free-draining
HARDINESS Z5–8 H8–3
FLOWERING Early and midsummer

RAISED PLANTING

Plants prone to rot at the base, and those with variegated foliage that tends to revert, are best planted with their crowns slightly above soil level.

Sisyrinchium striatum 'Aunt May' Satin flower

WITH VERTICAL, SWORD-SHAPED, variegated leaves about 16in (40cm) long, and stiff flower spikes with pale yellow flowers, 'Aunt May' is a very striking plant. The fan of evergreen leaves has an architectural symmetry and needs to be planted where it can be seen clearly, in free-draining soil with average fertility. Its parent, *Sisyrinchium striatum*, has plain green leaves. The semievergreen, 20in- (50cm-) high *S. graminoides* has blue flowers, and all varieties look good in gravel gardens.

OTHER VARIETIES *S.* 'Biscutella' (smaller-growing, heavily veined, dull yellow flowers); *S. californicum* (dark-veined, bright yellow flowers, gray-green leaves); *S. idahoense* 'Album' (smaller-growing, white flowers).

PLANT PROFILE	
HEIGHT To 20in (50cm)	
SPREAD 10in (25cm)	
SITE Full sun	
SOIL Average, free-draining	
HARDINESS Z7–8 H8–7	
FLOWERING Early and midsummer	

Smilacina racemosa False spikenard

THE FLUFFY WHITE FLOWERS of false spikenard appear in clusters at the ends of arching stems—not dangling all the way along them, as with Solomon's seal, to which this plant is sometimes likened. Being a woodland plant with spring flowers, it is perfect for shady, damp, rich soil, where it will form large clumps. The blooms can be used for cut-flower displays in the spring, or in autumn, when tiny green berries that ripen to red appear. Established clumps can be divided in the spring to create extra plants, but make sure each division has its own set of roots.

OTHER VARIETY *S. stellata* (tiny white, starlike flowers on arching stems, similar to *S. racemosa*).

PLANT PROFILE

HEIGHT 3ft (1m)

SPREAD 24in (60cm)

SITE Dappled or deep shade

SOIL Moist, fertile

HARDINESS Z4–9 H9–1

FLOWERING Mid- and late spring

S

Soldanella minima Least snowbell

THE LEAVES OF THIS PLANT are attractively rounded or heart-shaped, and the flower stems that rise through the foliage have downward-pointing, bell-shaped, pale blue (sometimes white) flowers. The plant dislikes very wet winters (it can be potted and kept in a cool greenhouse from the end of autumn to the following spring), and slugs and snails may attack the new growth. To help alleviate both problems, apply a layer of sand over the soil. This facilitates drainage and deters slugs, which dislike the sharp surface.

OTHER VARIETIES *S. alpina* (bluish violet flowers); *S. carpatica* (violet-blue flowers); *S. villosa* (larger-growing, violet flowers).

PLANT PROFILE	
HEIGHT 4in (10cm)	
SPREAD 8in (20cm)	
SITE Full sun	
SOIL Free-draining	
HARDINESS Z4–7 H7–1	
FLOWERING Early spring	

Soleirolia soleirolii Baby's tears

S

MAKING INCREDIBLY EFFECTIVE groundcover, this plant quickly sends out a thin, fast-spreading mat of small, fresh green leaves and will colonize any spare piece of ground, whether it is a slope or an area beneath trees. Baby's tears is tolerant of a wide range of soil conditions and will grow in either sun or shade. It is cut back by the frost, but quickly recovers the following spring in mild climates. Make sure you really do want baby's tears in your garden before planting it—once it takes hold, eradication is virtually impossible. Other varieties may be difficult to find.

OTHER VARIETIES *S. soleirolii* 'Aurea' (golden green leaves); *S. soleirolii* 'Variegata' (leaves with silver markings).

PLANT PROFILE
HEIGHT 2in (5cm)
SPREAD Indefinite
SITE Sun or shade
SOIL Average
HARDINESS Z10–15 H12–10
FLOWERING Summer

S | *Solidago* 'Goldenmosa' Goldenrod

THIS IS A VIGOROUS, LATE-SUMMER PLANT, and a good choice for lovers of bright yellow. It makes a bushy clump in borders or wild gardens, and you can use its multiplying tendency to create gradually spreading drifts. 'Golden Wings' is a tall alternative, at nearly 6ft (2m) high, while *Solidago virgaurea* subsp. *alpestris* var. *minutissima* is one of the shortest, growing 2–8in (5–20cm) high. All varieties prefer free-draining, sandy soil and full sun. One possible problem with this plant is powdery mildew, which can be reduced by watering the plant during the growing period.

OTHER VARIETY   *S.* 'Crown of Rays' (shorter, golden yellow flowers in flattened heads).

PLANT PROFILE
HEIGHT To 30in (75cm)
SPREAD 18in (45cm)
SITE Full sun
SOIL Average, free-draining
HARDINESS Z5–9 H9–5
FLOWERING Late summer and early autumn

x *Solidaster luteus* 'Lemore'

S

WITH ITS BRIGHT MASS of lemon yellow, daisylike flowers, this perennial looks good when planted toward the front of a border, where it adds pastel shades through the second half of summer and into the autumn. Darker, more intense adjacent colors provide an effective contrast, bringing out its gentle hue. The flowers also add an attractive note to a cut-flower arrangement. Soil with average fertility is perfectly acceptable, but good drainage is important, as is plenty of bright sun. 'Lemore' is sometimes prone to powdery mildew, but this can be prevented by watering during the growing season or treating it with an appropriate fungicide spray.

PLANT PROFILE

HEIGHT 32in (80cm)

SPREAD 32in (80cm)

SITE Full sun

SOIL Average, free-draining

HARDINESS Z4–9

FLOWERING Midsummer to early autumn

S | *Spartina pectinata* 'Aureomarginata' Prairie cord grass

IF YOU HAVE A PIECE OF SPARE GROUND near a pond, then this spreading, but easily controllable, grass may be for you. It thrives in moist soil, where it makes mounds of glossy, thin, olive green leaves with yellow stripes. It can also be grown on other sites, provided the soil does not dry out; away from wet ground its spread is reduced. The straw-colored flowers appear on tall spires and gradually turn brown, but the best reason for including this plant in a garden is its autumn foliage, which flares up yellow before fading to beige for the winter. If space permits, grow it in drifts—for example, by the edge of a stream, or in a coastal location, since it is tolerant of salt.

OTHER VARIETY *S. pectinata* (green leaves).

PLANT PROFILE
HEIGHT 4ft (1.2m)
SPREAD Indefinite
SITE Full sun
SOIL Wet
HARDINESS Z8–11 H12–8
FLOWERING Autumn

Stachys byzantina Lamb's ears

S

SOFT, SILKY, AND SILVERY GRAY, the leaves of this plant look and feel just like lambs' ears. Although the description of pink-purple flowers sounds attractive, in reality the blooms are not spectacular and many gardeners remove the flower stems so they will not detract from the foliage. Provide free-draining, average garden soil and full sun. *Stachys byzantina* 'Silver Carpet' is a good alternative because it very rarely flowers and the leaves have a strong silvery tinge.

OTHER VARIETIES *S. byzantina* 'Big Ears' (large, grayish white felted mid-green leaves); *S. byzantina* 'Cotton Boll' (clusters of modified flowers looking like cotton balls); *S. byzantina* 'Primrose Heron' (yellowish gray leaves).

PLANT PROFILE
HEIGHT 18in (45cm)
SPREAD 24in (60cm)
SITE Full sun
SOIL Average, free-draining
HARDINESS Z4–8 H8–1
FLOWERING Early summer to early autumn

Stipa calamagrostis Feather grass

THIS IS ONE OF THE BEST GRASSES for any medium-size garden. In summer, feather grass is beautifully graceful, with silvery flowers light enough to catch a passing breeze. By the end of the summer, the flowers have changed to fawn, and a few weeks later, in autumn, the foliage turns yellow and stays evergreen until really cold nights set in. It is also a wonderfully tactile plant and is best grown where you can flick it with your fingers as you pass, and use the flowers for cut-flower displays. Light, free-draining soil gives the best results.

OTHER VARIETIES *S. arundinacea* (feathery dark green leaves, streaked orange-brown); *S. gigantea* (larger-growing, silvery purplish green flower spikes turning gold).

PLANT PROFILE
HEIGHT 3ft (1m)
SPREAD 4ft (1.2m)
SITE Full sun
SOIL Fertile, free-draining
HARDINESS Z7–10
FLOWERING Summer

Strobilanthes attenuata (syn. *S. atropurpureus*)

GROWN FOR ITS QUIRKILY ATTRACTIVE, tubular flowers, about 1½in (4cm) long, this Indian perennial can be made even bushier by pinching out the growing tips in the spring. The indigo or purple flower color looks slightly richer and darker when seen in light shade. The soil needs to be light and free-draining for the plant to thrive and in cold-climate gardens it needs the protection of a thick cover of mulch around the plant in the winter. Most other *Strobilanthes* are tender and need to be grown in a cool greenhouse over winter—they can then be placed outside in the summer when the last frost is past.

PLANT PROFILE
HEIGHT 4ft (1.2m)
SPREAD 3ft (1m)
SITE Full sun or partial shade
SOIL Free-draining
HARDINESS Z5–9 H9–5
FLOWERING Summer

S | *Stylophorum diphyllum* Celandine poppy

THIS IS A BEAUTIFUL POPPY with distinctive and attractive, five- to seven-fingered leaves, which can grow to 12in (30cm) in length, and small yellow or orange flowers. While most poppies are sun-lovers, this type prefers moist but free-draining, leafy soil at the edge of a group of trees, or in a shrub border where it will benefit from some light shade. You can propagate it by collecting seed or by dividing large clumps in the autumn. Sometimes the pale yellow *Stylophorum lasiocarpum* is also sold in nurseries, but it is quite short-lived.

PLANT PROFILE	
HEIGHT 12in (30cm)	
SPREAD 12in (30cm)	
SITE Partial shade	
SOIL Moist but free-draining	
HARDINESS Z5–8 H8–1	
FLOWERING Late spring and summer	

Symphyandra wanneri

S

WITH FLOWERS A LITTLE LIKE those of a campanula (bellflower), to which it is related, this plant produces a good show of dark violet-blue blooms in summer. Sometimes taking a few years to flower, it often then dies, but it scatters so much seed that there will be plenty of replacements for the following spring. Move young plants to any gaps in the border where, being just knee-high or less, they need to be placed toward the front. Light, free-draining soil is best, but note that new growth acts as a magnet for slugs and snails.

OTHER VARIETIES *S. armena* (larger-growing, white or pale blue flowers); *S. hofmannii* (larger-growing, white to cream flowers); *S. pendula* (larger-growing, creamy white flowers).

PLANT PROFILE	
HEIGHT 12in (30cm)	
SPREAD 12in (30cm)	
SITE Full sun or light shade	
SOIL Free-draining	
HARDINESS Z7–9 H9–7	
FLOWERING Summer	

S *Symphytum* 'Goldsmith' Comfrey

IN THE WILDER PARTS of the garden, where the soil is moist and heavy, comfrey produces flowering, quick-spreading groundcover. Keep it out of formal borders, however, or it will overwhelm its neighbors. 'Goldsmith' has rich green leaves with cream and yellow or gold markings. Its foliage is so good, in fact, that this feature is more valued than the flowers. Once the flowers have faded, shear the plant to promote a second flush of leaves.

OTHER VARIETIES *S. caucasicum* (larger-growing, bright blue flowers, lance-shaped mid-green leaves); *S.* 'Hidcote Blue' (larger-growing, pale blue flowers from red buds, mid-green leaves); *S.* 'Hidcote Pink' (pale pink and white flowers, mid-green leaves).

PLANT PROFILE
HEIGHT 12in (30cm)
SPREAD 12in (30cm)
SITE Full sun or partial shade
SOIL Moist
HARDINESS Z5–9 H9–5
FLOWERING Mid- and late spring

Tanacetum coccineum 'James Kelway' Painted daisy

HELD HIGH ABOVE this plant's finely divided foliage are superb, rich crimson, daisylike flowers, each with a yellow eye. It offers a first-rate display in early summer borders, needing only bright sun and average soil to succeed, although the ground should be more on the light and free-draining side. Promptly deadhead fading flowers to encourage a second flush later in the summer. Excellent alternatives include the cerise-pink 'Brenda', pink 'Eileen May Robinson', and white 'Snow Cloud'.

OTHER VARIETIES *T. balsamita* (larger-growing, white flowers with yellow eyes); *T. parthenium* (smaller-growing, yellow and white flowers); *T. vulgare* (smaller-growing, clusters of bright yellow flowers).

PLANT PROFILE

HEIGHT 24in (60cm)

SPREAD 18in (45cm)

SITE Full sun

SOIL Average, free-draining

HARDINESS Z5–9 H9–5

FLOWERING Early summer

T

Telekia speciosa Large yellow ox-eye

THIS IS A FUN, SPREADING PERENNIAL with rather limp leaves, 12in (30cm) long, and tall stems bearing shaggy, daisylike flowers. *Telekia speciosa* is generally considered much too ungainly for the more manicured border, but it is extremely useful in cottage-style and wild gardens, as well as on the banks of streams, because it self-seeds so freely. It forms clumps, and can be positioned as a surprise feature in unlikely places—as a backdrop to the cardoon (*Cynara cardunculus*), for example—or in shady corners of the garden. Provide moist soil and some shelter in exposed, windy gardens, and take precautions against slugs.

PLANT PROFILE

HEIGHT To 6ft (2m)

SPREAD 3ft (1m)

SITE Partial shade

SOIL Moist

HARDINESS Z5–8 H8–5

FLOWERING Late summer and early autumn

Tellima grandiflora Fringe cups

HAPPY IN WOODLAND CONDITIONS, where self-seeding produces
good groundcover, as well as in the drier parts of a shrub border,
this is a dual-purpose plant. It has oval leaves, up to 4in (10cm)
wide, with tall stems of tiny greenish white flowers growing toward
the top. These open from small, tight buds to give an open, airy
display. Carefully dig up the seedlings in the spring and plant them
close together to create a clump of five or six plants in moist but
free-draining soil.

OTHER VARIETY *T. grandiflora* 'Purpurteppich' (smaller-growing,
pink-fringed green flowers, green leaves flushed purple-red).

PLANT PROFILE
HEIGHT To 32in (80cm)
SPREAD 12in (30cm)
SITE Partial shade
SOIL Moist, free-draining
HARDINESS Z4–8 H8–1
FLOWERING Late spring to midsummer

T *Thalictrum aquilegiifolium* Meadow rue

A SHOW OF DAINTY LEAVES and tiny, fluffy flowers (without petals) on angular stems give meadow rue an airy appearance. Rather than making a visual barrier, the plant's open tracery is see-through, so try placing it toward the front of a border with contrasting-colored plants behind. If a similar effect is required for the second half of summer, try *Thalictrum delavayi* 'Hewitt's Double', which has long-lasting mauve flowers. Moist soil is best for all meadow rues.

OTHER VARIETIES *T. aquilegiifolium* var. *album* (white flowers); *T. aquilegiifolium* 'Thundercloud' (dark purple flowers); *T. flavum* subsp. *glaucum* (sulfur yellow flowers, blue-gray leaves); *T. rochebruneanum* (white or lavender-pink flowers).

PLANT PROFILE

HEIGHT To 3ft (1m)

SPREAD 18in (45cm)

SITE Partial shade

SOIL Moist

HARDINESS Z5–9 H9–5

FLOWERING Early summer

Thalictrum flavum subsp. *glaucum* Yellow meadow rue

T

WITH ITS OPEN, AIRY STEMS and aerial show of tiny flowers, this meadow rue very is similar to *Thalictrum aquilegiifolium*. It is a good plant for the middle of a border in a cottage-style garden, or for a wild area or the dappled shade beneath deciduous trees. A dark background helps to show off the clouds of yellow flowers, but if there is anything behind it that has a similar color, then the hazy effect will be immediately lost. Plant it in moist soil that doesn't dry out, and divide clumps in the spring.

OTHER VARIETIES *T. delavayi* 'Album' (larger-growing, white flowers); *T. flavum* (fragrant, yellow and white flowers).

PLANT PROFILE
HEIGHT To 3ft (1m)
SPREAD 24in (60cm)
SITE Partial shade
SOIL Moist
HARDINESS Z6–8 H8–4
FLOWERING Summer

T *Thermopsis rhombifolia* var. *montana* False lupin

THE EARLY SUMMER BUZZ OF BEES accompanies the flowering of this plant, which has yellow, lupinlike blooms and three-fingered leaves. It is a bright, invasive plant and needs to be restricted to wild gardens—in a border, it will attempt to take over all available space. For a taller version, try the yellow-flowering *Thermopsis villosa*. Its blooms open slightly earlier, from the end of spring. Both are tough and sturdy survivors, tolerating a range of different garden sites and soils, although free-draining ground is best. Take care when planning its position because it does not like being moved once established.

OTHER VARIETY *L. villosa* (taller-growing, downy yellow flowers, blue-gray leaves).

PLANT PROFILE

HEIGHT 3ft (1m)

SPREAD 24in (60cm)

SITE Full sun or partial shade

SOIL Free-draining

HARDINESS Z3–8 H8–1

FLOWERING Early summer

Tiarella cordifolia Foam flower

T

PRODUCING A BOLD SHOW of 4in- (10cm-) long leaves, through which tall, thin stems appear holding creamy white flowers, this perennial is at its best in moist, fertile ground. In the wild, it is found in large colonies in woodlands, where it spreads by underground stems, and it is suitable for a similar site in the garden, wild areas, or a position close to natural ponds. *Tiarella wherryi* is more compact and a better choice for a smaller garden, while *T. wherryi* 'Bronze Beauty' offers an exciting contrast between its white flowers and dark reddish bronze leaves.

OTHER VARIETY *T.* 'Martha Oliver' (white flowers, leaves with maroon markings).

PLANT PROFILE

HEIGHT 4–12in (10–30cm)

SPREAD To 12in (30cm)

SITE Deep or light shade

SOIL Moist, fertile

HARDINESS Z3–7 H7–1

FLOWERING Late spring to midsummer

T *Tradescantia* Andersoniana Group 'Osprey' Spiderwort

EASILY GROWN AND CREATING COLORFUL DRIFTS, this is a clump-forming, hardy perennial (sometimes called spiderwort). Although sharing the same name, it is nothing like the trailing tradescantias popularly grown as houseplants. Either grow it in a single-color group or combine it with the dark blue 'Isis', whitish, pale blue 'Iris Pritchard', red 'Karminglut', or 'Purple Dome'. All are easily grown in moist but free-draining soil. If the soil is too rich there will be an abundance of lax, soft growth and fewer flowers.

OTHER VARIETIES (all Andersoniana Group) 'J.C. Weguelin' (large pale blue flowers); 'Purewell Giant' (smaller-growing, large purple to rose red flowers); 'Zwanenburg Blue' (large dark blue flowers).

PLANT PROFILE
HEIGHT 24in (60cm)
SPREAD 18in (45cm)
SITE Sun or light shade
SOIL Moist, free-draining
HARDINESS Z5–9 H9–5
FLOWERING Early summer to early autumn

Tricyrtis formosana Toad lily

T

THIS PLANT IS EXQUISITE and needs a position at the front of the border. The six small, open petals have beautiful markings, with tiny purple spots on a white background, and an erect, fleshy middle. Despite their exotic look, toad lilies are easy to grow, and given moist, rich soil they will spread to form decent groups. There are a few different types to choose from, all with different colored markings. Toad lilies dislike being moved once they are in the ground, and you will need to keep a close watch for slugs and snails.

OTHER VARIETIES *S. hirta* 'Alba' (green-flushed white flowers with pink-tinged centers); *S. hirta* 'Miyazaki' (white flowers with lilac purple spots); *T. macrantha* (deep yellow flowers with red-brown spots).

PLANT PROFILE	
HEIGHT To 32in (80cm)	
SPREAD 18in (45cm)	
SITE Deep or partial shade	
SOIL Moist, fertile	
HARDINESS Z6–9 H9–6	
FLOWERING Early autumn	

T | *Trifolium repens* 'Purpurascens Quadrifolium' Clover

WITH ITS SEMIEVERGREEN, BICOLORED leaves, purple-maroon in the middle and green all around the margins, this is a very special form of clover. It has an incredibly invasive nature, however, which means that the wildfower garden is the only place it can be safely grown. Don't be tempted to put it in your ornamental lawn—if you do, the smooth green grass will be quickly colonized by scores of maroon blobs. In summer it produces small, rounded white flowers.

OTHER VARIETIES *T. pratense* 'Susan Smith' (larger-growing, leaves with gold, veinlike markings); *T. repens* 'Green Ice' (gray-green leaves with a darker center); *T. repens* 'Purpurascens' (chocolate brown foliage, white flowers); *T. repens* 'Wheatfen' (maroon flowers and leaves).

PLANT PROFILE
HEIGHT To 4in (10cm)
SPREAD Indefinite
SITE Full sun
SOIL Moist but free-draining
HARDINESS Z4–8 H8–1
FLOWERING Summer

Trillium grandiflorum Wake robin

T

A GARDEN AREA WITH MOIST SOIL and dappled shade offers the perfect conditions for this groundcover plant. The leaves grow to 12in (30cm) long, and the yellow-eyed flowers, which gradually turn pink, sit flush with the top of the foliage. Enrich the ground with annual additions of leaf mold for the best results. *Trillium erectum* grows slightly taller and has deep reddish purple spring flowers (sometimes white or yellow). *T. sessile* is 12in (30cm) high with red–maroon flowers and 5in– (12cm–) long leaves.

OTHER VARIETIES *T. erectum* f. *albiflorum* (white or pale pink flowers); *T. grandiflorum* 'Flore Pleno' (double, white flowers); *T. luteum* (gold- or bronze-green flowers).

PLANT PROFILE

HEIGHT To 16in (40cm)

SPREAD 12in (30cm)

SITE Deep or partial shade

SOIL Moist, fertile

HARDINESS Z4–7 H7–3

FLOWERING Spring and summer

T *Trollius chinensis* 'Golden Queen' Globeflower

SOME OF THE BEST FLOWERS for the spring and early summer are provided by globeflowers with their buttercup-like yellow or orange blooms, held on long thin stems. 'Golden Queen' flowers slightly later than most, and has rich orange flowers, 2in (5cm) wide, with long petals. Other types also have excellent colors, such as the early-spring-flowering *Trollius* x *cultorum* 'Earliest of All' (yellow), and the late-spring 'Feuertroll' (rich orange-yellow). All like boggy, wet soil near a pond, or damp ground in a border.

OTHER VARIETIES *T.* x *cultorum* 'Alabaster' (primrose yellow flowers); *T.* x *cultorum* 'Lemon Queen' (pale yellow flowers); *T. europaeus* (lemon yellow flowers); *T. pumilus* (smaller-growing, gold-yellow flowers).

PLANT PROFILE
HEIGHT To 3ft (1m)
SPREAD 18in (45cm)
SITE Full sun or partial shade
SOIL Wet
HARDINESS Z3–7
FLOWERING Midsummer

Tulbaghia violacea Wild garlic

T

THIS GORGEOUS PLANT, with narrow, strap-shaped leaves and slim stems bearing up to 20 starlike flowers, requires very specific conditions. Originating from South Africa, it needs a sunny, sheltered position and moderately rich soil with very good drainage. In cold-climate gardens you should dig it up in autumn and keep it potted in a cool greenhouse until the following spring. Although not a member of the garlic family, its characteristic smell gives rise to its common name of wild garlic. An alternative is *Tulbaghia violacea* 'Silver Lace', which has cream-colored striped leaves and larger flowers. Both types grow into attractive clumps.

OTHER VARIETY *T. simmleri* (fragrant, deep purple flowers).

PLANT PROFILE
HEIGHT 18–24in (45–60cm)
SPREAD 10in (25cm)
SITE Full sun
SOIL Free-draining
HARDINESS Z7–10 H10–7
FLOWERING Midsummer to early autumn

U | *Uncinia rubra* Hook sedge

NATIVE TO THE MOUNTAINS of New Zealand, this evergreen sedge has narrow, slow-growing, reddish brown leaves that are at their most attractive in the spring and early summer. It develops into a decent clump, but the flowers are totally insignificant, not least because they are the same color as the foliage. The seed of the hook sedge is interesting, though; each one has a tiny hook that latches onto any passing animal, thereby aiding dispersion. You can grow hook sedge in a sunny position and moist but well-drained soil, perhaps close to a natural pond.

OTHER VARIETY *U. uncinata* (pale brown to red-brown, flat, leaves with rough margins, spikes of dark brown flowers).

PLANT PROFILE	
HEIGHT	12in (30cm)
SPREAD	14in (35cm)
SITE Full sun or light shade	
SOIL Moist but free-draining	
HARDINESS Z8–11	
FLOWERING Mid- and late summer	

Uvularia grandiflora Merrybells

U

A NORTH AMERICAN WOODLAND PLANT, merrybells happily makes the transition to garden conditions and thrives if given rich, moist but well-drained soil. It is ideal for an area close to a natural pond, where it will form open clumps and provide a good place for toads and frogs to hide. It can also be grown in borders, but the soil must be moist, with plenty of leaf mold added to it. In midspring, merrybells is topped by downward-pointing, 2in- (5cm-) long yellow flowers. Beware of attacks from slugs and snails when the new, fresh green growth emerges in the early spring.

PLANT PROFILE	
HEIGHT 30in (75cm)	
SPREAD 12in (30cm)	
SITE Deep or partial shade	
SOIL Fertile, moist but free-draining	
HARDINESS Z3–7 H7–1	
FLOWERING Mid- and late spring	

V | *Valeriana phu* 'Aurea' Valerian

IN SPRING THIS PLANT DELIVERS A LOVELY SURPRISE, when its young foliage emerges a buttery yellow. After this eye-catching show, the leaves mature to lime green, then mid-green by summer. To achieve the brightest possible spring foliage, grow the plant in a sunny spot in moist but free-draining soil. If grown among spring bulbs, especially white-flowering ones with just a hint of blue, 'Aurea' will put on a strong show. By comparison, the early summer flowers, which are white, are fairly unremarkable and just a little disappointing. On a windy site, you will need to provide a strong support to keep the plant upright.

OTHER VARIETY *V. officinalis* (larger growing, bright green leaves).

PLANT PROFILE

HEIGHT 5ft (1.5m)

SPREAD 24in (60cm)

SITE Full sun or dappled shade

SOIL Moist but free-draining

HARDINESS Z5–9 H9–5

FLOWERING Early summer

Vancouveria hexandra Inside-out flower

V

A WOODLAND GARDEN is the perfect setting for this creeping, deciduous perennial, which will thrive in the light shade and rich, moist but free-draining soil. A wonderful groundcover plant, it will also do well in the shady, wilder edges of a more formal setting. Near the base of the plant the shapely leaves can reach 18in (45cm) long; toward the top, they gradually decrease in size to just 3in (8cm). As spring turns to summer, airy clusters of tiny white flowers appear on long leafless stems (*see inset*).

OTHER VARIETY *V. chrysantha* (smaller-growing, yellow flowers and glossy, leathery, dark green leaves; can be very invasive).

PLANT PROFILE

HEIGHT 16in (40cm)

SPREAD 16in (40cm)

SITE Partial shade

SOIL Moist but free-draining

HARDINESS Z5–8 H8–5

FLOWERING Late spring and early summer

V | *Veratrum nigrum* Black false hellebore

FROM A DENSE ROSETTE OF LONG, PLEATED LEAVES, this architectural plant sends up a tall flower stem packed with branches of tiny, dark red-brown flowers. Enjoy the effect, but don't get too close, because they carry an unpleasant smell. Unless you can give it a light background the intensity of the flower color will be lost; in a darker setting, the green-white flowers of *Veratrum album* are more visually pleasing. All veratrums need a sheltered position with rich, moist but well-drained soil. Full sun isn't a problem, as long as you don't allow the ground to dry out. You can raise plants from seed, but you will have to wait five or six years for the first flush of flowers.

OTHER VARIETY *V. viride* (a taller plant with yellowish green flowers).

PLANT PROFILE

HEIGHT 24–48in (60–120cm)

SPREAD 24in (60cm)

SITE Partial shade

SOIL Fertile, moist but free-draining

HARDINESS Z6–9 H9–6

FLOWERING Mid- to late summer

Verbascum chaixii 'Album' Nettle-leaved mullein

THE TALL, SHOWY SPIRES of 'Album' are dotted along their length with white, saucer-shaped flowers, each with a mauve eye. A well-loved cottage garden plant, it makes a graceful addition to the summer border. Planted in a group or drift, it looks particularly impressive against the dark background of a beech hedge. Mulleins do best in well-drained, average soil; in richer soils they will grow too tall and require staking. There are many excellent yellow-flowering types, including the 4ft (1.2m) *Verbascum* 'Cotswold Queen' and *V.* 'Gainsborough'. For extra height, grow *V. olympicum,* at 6ft (2m), and *V. bombyciferum,* at about the same height.

OTHER VARIETY *V. chaixii* 'Pink Domino' (taller, rose pink flowers).

PLANT PROFILE

HEIGHT 3ft (1m)

SPREAD 18in (45cm)

SITE Full sun

SOIL Average, free-draining

HARDINESS Z5–8

FLOWERING Mid- to late summer

V

Verbascum 'Helen Johnson' Mullein

WITH THEIR REGAL FLOWER SPIRES, mulleins add a touch of elegance to cottage garden and border plans. Strong yellows abound, but 'Helen Johnson', a fairly recent introduction, comes in a more subtle color that is ideal for low-key arrangements. Delightful, pinkish brown flowers, with a center of rich purple filaments, appear from early to late summer on 18in- (45cm-) long branched spikes. A rosette of evergreen, gray-green, downy leaves at the base of the plant sets them off nicely. It will perform best on poor, well-drained soil in full sun; on richer soils it will grow taller and require staking.

OTHER VARIETY *V. phoeniceum* (taller-growing, white, pink, or violet to dark purple flowers).

PLANT PROFILE

HEIGHT 3ft (1m)

SPREAD 12in (30cm)

SITE Full sun

SOIL Free-draining

HARDINESS Z6–9 H9–5

FLOWERING Early to late summer

Choose a healthy, nonflowering stem to use as a cutting. To increase the number of cuttings, divide each stem into roughly equal sections.

Verbena bonariensis Purpletop vervain

V

THE ULTIMATE "SEE-THROUGH" PLANT, *Verbena bonariensis* has an open habit that can be used to great effect toward the front of a border. By thinning out some of the more dense central growth, you can further enhance the hazelike effect of the tall stems and airy flowerheads. In terms of providing valuable height, shape, and color, it is hard to beat. Free-draining soil suits it best, but it will survive in heavier ground. In colder areas, cut stems back in autumn and keep plants potted in a cool greenhouse until spring.

OTHER VARIETIES *V. corymbosa* (red-purple flowers); *V. hastata* (violet to pink flowers).

PLANT PROFILE

HEIGHT To 6ft (2m)

SPREAD 18in (45cm)

SITE Full sun

SOIL Free-draining

HARDINESS Z7–11 H12–7

FLOWERING Midsummer to early autumn

V *Vernonia noveboracensis* Ironweed

THE IMPOSING HEIGHT OF THIS PLANT makes it a useful, and very colorful, addition to the back of the border. Ironweed is topped by fluffy heads of rich red-purple or white tubular flowers. It is easy to grow and requires only moderately fertile, free-draining soil. Even though the stems are sturdy and normally self-supporting, in exposed, windy gardens staking may be necessary. These plants self-seed quite freely, so if you don't want ironweed growing all over the garden, cut off the flowers as soon as they start to fade.

OTHER VARIETY *V. crinita* (similar with red-brown flowers).

PLANT PROFILE

HEIGHT 6ft (2m)

SPREAD 24in (60cm)

SITE Full sun or partial shade

SOIL Moderately fertile, free-draining

HARDINESS Z4–8 H8–3

FLOWERING Late summer to midautumn

CREEPING ROOTSTOCK

You can make new plants by cutting lengths of root into sections, each with its own root system and a strongly growing bud.

Veronica austriaca subsp. *teucrium* 'Crater Lake Blue' Speedwell

V

THERE ARE MANY SPEEDWELLS, all bearing candlelike spikes of saucer-shaped flowers that stand erect above the foliage, but 'Crater Lake Blue' produces one of the best blues. ('Kapitän' and 'Shirley Blue' are good runners-up.) Useful in formal borders and cottage gardens, it makes a wonderful sight growing in a circle around a feature plant, such as *Verbascum olympicum*, with its tall spikes of yellow flowers. As the plant matures, the soft grayish green leaves grow together to form a compact mound.

OTHER VARIETIES *V. gentianoides* 'Variegata' (blue flowers, white-variegated leaves); *V. longifolia* (larger-growing, lilac-blue flowers); *V. spicata* subsp. *incana* 'Wendy' (bright blue flowers, gray leaves).

PLANT PROFILE

HEIGHT 12in (30cm)

SPREAD 16in (40cm)

SITE Full sun or partial shade

SOIL Average, free-draining

HARDINESS Z6–8 H8–6

FLOWERING Summer

V *Veronicastrum virginicum album* Culver's root

A CHARMING SUMMER-FLOWERING PLANT that is similar to veronica, only taller. Rising out of whorls of dark green leaves, tall, feathery, white flower spikes make it a good match with other upright plants for the back of a mixed border. It will also look imposing erupting from a carpet of rounded, lower-growing subjects. White is an extremely versatile color and can be slotted in anywhere—among a blaze of hothouse shades or a palette of pastels. It is generally an unfussy plant but moderately fertile, moist soil is best. One drawback is that it is prone to attacks of powdery mildew.

OTHER VARIETIES *V. virginicum* 'Apollo' (light pink flowers); *V. virginicum* 'Fascination' (pale rose flowers).

PLANT PROFILE

HEIGHT 6ft (2m)

SPREAD 18in (45cm)

SITE Full sun or partial shade

SOIL Moderately fertile, moist

HARDINESS Z3–8 H8–1

FLOWERING Midsummer to early autumn

Viola riviniana Purpurea Group Common dog violet

V

TYPICALLY FOUND IN WOODLANDS, often at the base of hedgerows, the common dog violet is mostly grown as an attractive gap-filler in a wild garden. It tends to be invasive and is best kept out of borders. The beautiful pale-colored flowers, which carry a distinctive spur, can be encouraged to produce a second flush by gently trimming the plant after flowering. Like most violas, it does best in rich, moist soil. Other violas have their main flowering period during summer, when they make an excellent show among roses.

OTHER VARIETIES *V. cornuta* (smaller-growing, violet to lilac-blue flowers with white markings); *V.* 'Huntercombe Purple' (deep violet-blue flowers); *V. odorata* (fragrant, blue or white flowers).

PLANT PROFILE
HEIGHT 4–8in (10–20cm)
SPREAD 8–16in (20–40cm)
SITE Deep or partial shade
SOIL Moist, fertile
HARDINESS Z5–8 H8–5
FLOWERING Late spring and early summer

W | *Waldsteinia ternata* Siberian barren strawberry

THE SMALL, OPEN FLOWERS of this woodland native are set off beautifully by the contrasting dark green, semievergreen leaves. In dry shady areas, this quick-growing groundcover plant will produce a welcome burst of color at the end of spring. A woodland setting in moderately fertile, well-drained soil suits it best. Good drainage is a must, and heavy, wet ground must be avoided. Given the right conditions, there's a tendency for it to become invasive, so make sure it's not too close to any attractive neighbors that could get swamped. Propagating new plants by taking divisions in early spring is simple and very successful.

OTHER VARIETY *W. ternata* 'Variegata' (brighter leaves).

PLANT PROFILE
HEIGHT 4in (10cm)
SPREAD 24in (60cm)
SITE Full or partial shade
SOIL Moderately fertile, free-draining
HARDINESS Z3–8 H8–1
FLOWERING Late spring and early summer

Zantedeschia aethiopica 'Crowborough' Arum lily

SHAPELY WHITE SPATHES with a prominent yellow spike and luxuriant, glossy green leaves up to 16in (40cm) long give this plant a tropical feel. It makes an eye-catching display for the margins of a natural pond, where, as its roots work their way down into the mud, it will form large clumps. It can also be grown in large containers in a formal pond. It is very similar to its parent, *Zantedeschia aethiopica*, but is slightly hardier. As a marginal plant it can be submerged up to a depth of 12in (30cm). Plants growing close to or above the water line will need a protective winter mulch during cold spells.

OTHER VARIETY *Z. aethiopica* 'Green Goddess' (green spathes with a white center).

PLANT PROFILE	
HEIGHT	3ft (1m)
SPREAD	24in (60cm)
SITE	Full sun
SOIL	Wet
HARDINESS	Z8–10 H10–8
FLOWERING	Late spring to midsummer

A

Adriatic bellflower 65
African daisy 226
African lily 23
alkanet, green 237
allium 48, 175
alpine bells 93
anchusa 32, 39
anemone, false 35
angelica, Korean 36
angel's fishing rod 110
anise hyssop 24
arum, dragon 115
arum lily 315
asphodel 48
aster 177
   frost 51
   New England 50
autumn snakeroot 87
avens 147

B

baby's breath 153
baby's tears 279
balloon flower 248
balm
   bastard 211
   lemon 210
baneberry, red 20
barrenwort 122
bastard balm 211
bayonet plant 18
beardtongue 236
bear's breeches 16
bee blossom 142
bellflower
   Adriatic 65
   clustered 66
   gland 21
   Korean 66
   milky 67
   nettle-leaved 67
bergamot 217
blackberry lily 56

black-eyed Susan 263
black false hellebore 306
blanket flower 139
bleeding heart 108
bloody cranesbill 146
bluebells 113, 141
blue fescue 134
blue oat grass 160
blue star 30
blue switch grass 231
Bowles' golden grass 213
Bowles' golden sedge 70
bowman's root 148
box, clipped 155
bridal wreath 138
bronze fennel 136
brook saxifrage 59
brook thistle 88
bugle 25
bugloss
   giant viper's 118
   Italian 32
   Siberian 61
burnet 267
burning bush 109
bush clover 182
buttercups 33, 80, 258

C

calamint, lesser 63
candelabra primrose 252
cardinal flower 193
cardoon 99, 290
carnation 106
catmint 220
celandine
   greater 80
   lesser 258
   poppy 286
chameleon plant 170
chamomile 78
chervil, hairy 77
chicory 86
Chinese foxglove 259
Chinese lantern 245

Chinese rhubarb 260
chocolate cosmos 95
chrysanthemum 83
cinquefoil 251
clematis 34
clover 298
   bush 182
club-rush 270
clustered bellflower 66
cobra lily, striped 40
colewort 96
comfrey 288
common dog violet 313
common quaking grass 60
common reed 243
coneflower 116, 263
cosmos 34
   chocolate 95
cow parsley 38, 77
cowslip, giant 253
cranesbill 126
   bloody 146
crocosmia 75, 98
crosswort 244
cuckoo flower 68
culver's root 312
Cupid's dart 71

D

dahlia 102, 177, 182
daisy
   African 226
   Michaelmas 50
   painted 289
   shaster 183
dandelion, pink 97
day flower 89
daylily 163
deadnettle 179
delphinium 17, 104
digger's speedwell 234
dog's-tooth violet 129
dragon arum 115

E

elephant's ears 57
eulalia grass 214
evening primrose 223

F

fairy bells 112
false anemone 35
false indigo 55
false lily-of-the-valley 204
false lupin 294
false spikenard 277
feather grass 284
featherleaf Rodgers flower
    262
feather reed grass 62
fennel
    bronze 136
    Florence 136
    giant 133
fescue, blue 134
flax
    flowering 191
    New Zealand 242
    perennial 191
fleabane 124
Florence fennel 136
flowering flax 191
foam flower 295
foxglove 111
    Chinese 259
foxtail grass 27
foxtail lily 123
fringe cups 291
frost aster 51
fumitory 94

G

gardener's garters 239
garlic, wild 301
gaura 142
gayfeather 185
geranium 126, 144, 145,
    146

giant cowslip 253
giant fennel 133
giant marsh marigold 64
giant reed 46
giant rhubarb 152
giant scabious 75
giant viper's bugloss 118
ginger lily 156, 177
gland bellflower 21
glaucous hair grass 178
globe thistle 117
globeflower 300
gloxinia, hardy 173
goat's beard 45
goat's rue 140
golden groundsel 187
golden Japanese forest grass
    155
golden marguerite 37
golden ray 188
goldenrod 280
goldenstar 84
golden yarrow 125
grama, blue 58
granny's bonnet 39
grass 34, 58, 119, 155, 160,
    214, 282
    blue oat 160
    blue switch 231
    Bowles' golden 213
    common quaking 60
    eulalia 214
    feather 284
    foxtail 27
    golden Japanese forest 155
    glaucous hair 178
    Japanese blood 172
    lyme 184
    orchard 101
    Oriental fountain 235
    pampas 82, 92, 243
    plumed tussock 82
    prairie cord 282
    purple moor 215
    ravenna 264
    red switch 231
    ribbon 239

squirrel tail 168
tufted hair 105
    see also reed grass;
        sedge
greater celandine 80
ground elder, variegated
    22
groundsel
    golden 187
    showy 274
gunnera 53, 152

H

hairy chervil 77
hardy gloxinia 173
hellebore 162
    black false 306
heron's bill 126
Himalayan blue poppy 206
Himalayan parsley 273
hollyhock 17
honesty, perennial 194
honey bush 208
hook sedge 302
hosta 154, 169
hound's tongue 100
hydrangea 34

I

indigo, false 55
inside-out flower 305
ironweed 310
Italian bugloss 32

J

Jacob's ladder 249
Japanese anemone 34
Japanese blood grass 172
Japanese spurge 229
Jerusalem cross 197
Joe Pye weed 130

K

kingcup 64

king's spear 47
knapweed 72
knapweed, mountain 73
knotweed 238
Korean angelica 36
Korean bellflower 66

L

lady's mantle 26
lamb's ears 283
large yellow ox-eye 290
leadwort 76
least snowbell 278
lemon balm 210
leopard's bane 114
lesser calamint 63
lesser celandine 258
lily
    African 23
    arum 315
    blackberry 56
    foxtail 123
    ginger 156, 177
    paradise 233
    Peruvian 28
    striped cobra 40
    toad 297
    see also daylily; lilyturf
lily-of-the-valley 90
    false 204
lilyturf 192, 225
liverwort 164
loosestrife 200, 201
    purple 202
lords and ladies 44
lungwort 256
lupin 195
    false 294
lyme grass 184

M

Macedonian scabious 176
mallow 181
    musk 205
    prairie 275
marguerite, golden 37

marsh marigold, giant 64
masterwort 54
meadow rue 292
melick, Siberian 209
merrybells 303
Michaelmas daisy 50
milky bellflower 67
mint, pineapple 212
money plant 194
monkshood 19
montbretia 98
mountain knapweed 73
mouse plant 41
mugwort, western 43
mullein 307, 308
    nettle-leaved 307
musk mallow 205

N

navelwort 224
nettle-leaved bellflower 67
nettle-leaved mullein 307
New England aster 50
New Zealand flax 242
New Zealand satin flower 186

O

obedient plant 246
orchard grass 101
Oriental fountain grass 235
Oriental poppy 232
ox eye 17, 161
    large yellow 290

P

painted daisy 289
pampas grass 82, 92, 243
paradise lily 233
parsley, Himalayan 273
pasque flower 257
pearl everlasting 31
peony 230
perennial flax 191

perennial honesty 194
perennial phlox 241
periwinkle, lesser 84
Peruvian lily 28
phlox, perennial 241
pineapple mint 212
pincushion flower 269
pinks 106
plumed tussock grass 82
pokeweed 247
poppy 17
    celandine 286
    Himalayan blue 206
    Oriental 232
    plume 203
    snow 120
    Tibetan blue 206
    Welsh 207
    yellow horned 151
prairie cord grass 282
prairie mallow 275
primrose 33
    evening 223
primula 254
    candelabra 252
purple loosestrife 202
purple moor grass 215
purpletop vervain 309

Q

quaking grass, common 60
queen of the prairie 135

R

ravenna grass 264
red-hot poker 159, 177
red-hot-poker primula
    254
red switch grass 231
red valerian 74
reed
    common 243
    giant 46
reed grass, feather 62
rhubarb

Chinese 260
giant 152
ribbon grass 239
rocket, sweet 165
Rodgers flower
featherleaf 262
shieldleaf 53
rose campion 198
rosefoot 261
rudbeckia 177
rue
goat's 140
meadow 292
yellow 293
rye, wild 119

S

sage, sticky Jerusalem 240
salvia 265, 266
satin flower 276
New Zealand 186
saxifrage, brook 59
scabious
giant 75
Macedonian 176
sea holly 127, 208
sea lavender 189
sea oats 79
sea thrift 42
sedge 69, 70
Bowles' golden 70
hook 302
self-heal 255
shamrock 227
shasta daisy 183
shieldleaf Rodgers flower 53
shirane-aoi 150
shooting stars 113
showy groundsel 274
Siberian barren strawberry
314
Siberian bugloss 61
Siberian melick 209
silver spear 49
skunk cabbage 271
yellow 199

snakeroot, autumn 87
sneezewort 157
snowbell, least 278
snow-in-summer 100
snow poppy 120
snowy woodrush 196
solomon's seal 250
sow thistle 85
speedwell 311
digger's 234
spiderwort 296
spikenard, false 277
spring vetchling 180
spurge 131, 132
Japanese 229
squirrel tail grass 168
St. John's wort 171
sticky Jerusalem sage 240
stonecrop 272
strawberry 137
Siberian barren 314
striped cobra lily 40
sunflower 158
sweet pea 180
sweet rocket 165
sweet woodruff 141

T

thistle
brook 88
globe 117
Tibetan blue poppy 206
tickweed 91
toadflax 190
toad lily 297
tobacco plant 221
tufted hair grass 105
tulips 48, 175
tumbling Ted 268
turtlehead 81
twinspur 107

U

umbrella plant 103

V

valerian 304
red 74
vancouveria 305
variegated ground elder 22
verbena 197, 309
vervain, purpletop 309
vetchling, spring 180
violet
common dog 313
dog's-tooth 129
viper's bugloss, giant 118

W

wake robin 299
wallflower 128
water celery 222
water figwort 271
water forget-me-nots 271
Welsh poppy 207
western mugwort 43
whorlflower 218
wild garlic 301
wild rye 119
willow gentian 143
willow herb 121
windflower 33
woodruff, sweet 141
woodrush, snowy 196

Y

yarrow 17
golden 125
yellow horned poppy 151
yellow rue 293
yellow skunk cabbage 199

The publisher would like to thank the following for their kind permission to reproduce their photographs:

a=above; c=c̲ ̲ ̲ ̲ ̲ ̲l̲o̲w̲; l=left; r=right; t=top

A-Z Botanical Collection:
Mrs Ailsa M. Allaby 245br; John Arnold 85c; Ron Bass 86c; J.Brunsdon Rapkins 114c, 117c; Sue Cunningham Photographic 56br; James Guilliam 104c; David Hughes 215c; Jiri Loun 233c; Glenis Moore 171c; Adrian Thomas 140c 203c, 209c, 219c, 227c, 250c, 296c; Chris Wheeler 42c; Archie Young 65c

Blooms of Bressingham: 159c

Garden Picture Library:
Sunniva Harte 61c; Neil Holmes 6tr; Howard Rice 6l; JS Sira 7tl

Garden and Wildlife Matters:
101c

Garden World Images:
6br, 33c, 33br, 184c, 195c, 202c

Holt Studios International:
Helmut Partsch 278c; M. Szadzuik/ R. Zinck 289c

Photos Horticultural:
21c, 31c, 56c, 59c, 60c, 120c, 157c, 158c, 166c, 178c, 181c, 213c, 300c, 301c, 308c, 308r; ACM 91c, 245c; AGM 281c

Plant Pictures World Wide:
272c

Royal Botanic Garden, Edinburgh:
179c

Roger Smith/DK:
2c, 4c, 19c, 32tr, 32c, 47tr, 47c, 50tr, 51c, 64c, 71c, 74c, 75c, 82c, 95c, 98c, 99tr, 103c, 108tr, 121c, 128r, 135c, 136c, 144c, 145c, 146c, 154c, 162c, 164c, 172c, 172r, 198c, 210c, 212tr, 212c, 225c, 234c, 240c, 240r, 246c, 254c, 255c, 267c, 285tr, 288c, 313c, 315tr

Adrian Thomas:
269c, 224c

Steven Wooster:
"Elevation" garden for Chelsea Flower Show 2002 by Eric Demaeifer and Jane Hudson 7br

James Young:
37c, 48c, 99c, 118tr, 118c, 138c,152c, 160c, 206c, 239c, 244c, 247br, 252c, 261c, 283c, 292c.

All other images © Dorling Kindersley.

For further information see:
www.dkimages.com

Dorling Kindersley would also like to thank the following:
Helen Fewster and Letitia Luff for their editorial assistance; Kathie Gill for the index; and Archie Clapton in Media Resources.